Hellenic Studies 55

LOVING HUMANITY, LEARNING,
AND BEING HONORED

Recent Titles in the Hellenic Studies Series

Homer's Versicolored Fabric
The Evocative Power of Ancient Greek Epic Word-Making

Christianity and Hellenism in the Fifth-Century Greek East
Theodoret's Apologetics against the Greeks in Context

The Master of Signs
Signs and the Interpretation of Signs in Herodotus' Histories

The Epic Rhapsode and His Craft
Homeric Performance in a Diachronic Perspective

Eve of the Festival
Making Myth in Odyssey 19

Kleos in a Minor Key
The Homeric Education of a Little Prince

Plato's Counterfeit Sophists

Multitextuality in Homer's Iliad
The Witness of the Ptolemaic Papyri

Tragedy, Authority, and Trickery
The Poetics of Embedded Letters in Josephus

A Californian Hymn to Homer

Pindar's Verbal Art
An Ethnographic Study of Epinician Style

Iliad 10 and the Poetics of Ambush

The New Sappho on Old Age
Textual and Philosophical Issues

Hippota Nestor

Homer the Classic

Recapturing a Homeric Legacy
Images and Insights from the Venetus A Manuscript of the Iliad

http://chs.harvard.edu/chs/publications

LOVING HUMANITY, LEARNING, AND BEING HONORED

THE FOUNDATIONS OF LEADERSHIP IN XENOPHON'S *EDUCATION OF CYRUS*

Norman B. Sandridge

CENTER FOR HELLENIC STUDIES
Trustees for Harvard University
Washington, D.C.
Distributed by Harvard University Press
Cambridge, Massachusetts, and London, England
2012

Loving Humanity, Learning, and Being Honored: The Foundations of Leadership in Xenophon's Education of Cyrus by Norman B. Sandridge
Copyright © 2012 Center for Hellenic Studies, Trustees for Harvard University
All Rights Reserved.
Published by Center for Hellenic Studies, Trustees for Harvard University, Washington, D.C.
Distributed by Harvard University Press, Cambridge, Massachusetts, and London, England
Production: Kristin Murphy Romano
Cover design and illustration: Joni Godlove
Printed by Edwards Brothers, Inc., Ann Arbor, MI

LIBRARY OF CONGRESS CATALOGING-IN-PUBLICATION DATA

Sandridge, Norman B.
Loving humanity, learning, and being honored : the foundations of leadership in Xenophon's Education of Cyrus / by Norman B. Sandridge.
pages. cm. -- (Hellenic studies ; 55)
ISBN 978-0-674-06702-8 (alk. paper)
1. Xenophon. Cyropaedia. 2. Leadership. I. Title. II. Series: Hellenic studies ; 55.

PA4494.C9S26 2012
883'.01--dc23

2012024440

Acknowledgements

THE FOLLOWING STUDY is to some extent the result of a long interest in ancient leadership and the emotions. Thus I owe a debt of gratitude to many more friends and mentors than I have space to mention here, including to Dick Gerberding, who converted me to Classics from a budding career in physics, and to Stephen Sandridge, who from my early adolescence showed a Cambyses-like patience and generosity toward my persistent and sometimes forward questions about the character and behavior of others—even his own.

But for the composition of this book I must recognize the friendship and support of my colleagues at Howard University, who over the past several years either read the manuscript in its entirety or listened to my ideas and gave helpful feedback: Matt Amati, David Carlisle, John Chesley, Caroline Dexter, Rudolph Hock, Molly Levine, Arti Mehta, Lee Patterson. I am also grateful to my many colleagues in the field who read drafts, listened to presentations, engaged in dialogue, and challenged me to see Xenophon's Cyrus from perspectives entirely new to me: Emily Baragwanath, Jeff Beneker, Angelos Chaniotis, Sarah Ferrario, Johannes Haubold, David Konstan, Patrick Miller, Bill Race, Claire Taylor. Thanks are also due to Dan Joseph and Robin Olson, whose copy-edits significantly improved the style, clarity, and concision of this manuscript. This book is far better for their insights and suggestions, but I am fully responsible for any and all of the ways in which a scholarly work might be flawed.

I also wish to thank Harvard University's Center for Hellenic Studies in Washington, DC for a fellowship that afforded me the opportunity to compose this book in the recreational beauty of its library and grounds. I thank especially the director of the Center, Gregory Nagy, for his infectious ebullience and unwavering encouragement. I thank also the library staff for their expert and friendly help in navigating the library's world-class resources: Erika Bainbridge, Sophie Boisseau, Temple Wright.

Thanks are due to Jill Curry Robbins for her timely and efficient guidance through every stage of the publication process, including her expertise in art history, which helped me select what I believe is a cover image rich in color and meaning.

Finally, I dedicate this book to my wife Kimberly Judge Sandridge. It would be embarrassing and out of place for me to explain the reasons. Suffice it to say that in this life I've seen everything I can see, but I've never seen nothing like her.

Contents

Introduction

The Narrative

THE *EDUCATION OF CYRUS* OR *CYROPAEDIA* (c. 365 BCE) is, in broad terms, a simple narrative; its parts are few and clearly demarcated, its progression often predictable. Xenophon begins with the reflection that all governments, whether democratic, oligarchic, monarchic, or tyrannical, eventually collapse. He almost concludes that it is easier for someone to rule all other animals than human beings. But then he recalls the glorious career of Cyrus, who for much of his life led many nations of diverse ethnic and linguistic backgrounds. Xenophon then processes in loose chronology with Cyrus' biography, including his lineage, nature, and education. In Book One, he describes this education in three parts. As a youth in the Persian educational system, Cyrus learns the skills of the hunt as well as several moral virtues (self-restraint, justice, gratitude). He then travels to the Medan court of his grandfather, Astyages, where his virtues are put to the test. He also learns to ride a horse and to dress finely. In time, Cyrus returns to Persia to prepare for a military campaign against the Assyrians. There he participates in a lengthy dialogue with his father, Cambyses, to hone his understanding of the finer points of leadership. In particular he learns that it is acceptable to apply his hunting skills in the theater of war; enemies may be subjected to deceptive predation (though Cyrus turns out to have a knack for converting enemies into friends and willing followers).

From Book Two to the middle of Book Seven, Cyrus campaigns against the Assyrians and wins many allies along the way, including the Armenians, Cadusians, and Hyrcanians, as well as some noble Assyrians. His adventures may be thought of as the "application" of the many lessons in leadership he had learned in his youth. After the middle of Book Seven, Cyrus becomes ruler of Babylon (539 BCE). Eventually Cyrus *inherits* the Medan Empire, whereas in all other accounts Cyrus overtakes the Medes by war.[1] From this point Cyrus no

---

[1] Briant 1996:31–33.

longer operates as a military commander but as an administrator and figure-head. The newly-conquered Babylon, in particular, is most hostile to him, and so the modes of leadership he exhibits diverge somewhat from those in previous books but still resonate with earlier lessons. Cyrus himself now attempts to teach these precepts to others. The *Education of Cyrus* concludes in a way that many have seen as problematic: despite his best efforts to educate his sons to follow the example of his virtuous reign, Cyrus can prevent neither their bitter rivalry nor the decline of Persian culture. He dies "happy" from his own perspective, though perhaps not fully in the Solonic sense.[2]

Education, application, degeneration—*The End*. A simple narrative.

Interest in Xenophon's Cyrus

If we begin with the popular assumption that Xenophon wrote the *Cyropaedia* in order to talk about leadership,[3] we can offer many reasons why he might choose Cyrus as his subject. For one, Cyrus was already a famous figure in Greece, having established and then governed the Persian Empire almost two hundred years before Xenophon wrote his *Education* (559–530 BCE). Many Ionian Greek authors had already written accounts of Persian history (so-called *Persica*), and Xenophon would have had much material to work with, especially from the historian Herodotus and the court-physician-turned-historian Ctesias.[4] The distance in time also afforded the opportunity to embellish, omit, rework, or invent material as necessary, though it is also possible to see Xenophon as "correcting" other versions of a story. The fact that Cyrus was a Persian *barbaros*, a non-Greek, allowed Xenophon to study and celebrate him in ways that would be less politically controversial than if he had written, say, *The Education of Pericles*. Cyrus' "otherness" may have freed Xenophon to think in a livelier, less conventional, more theoretical fashion, to let his fantasies of the best form of leadership take hold. If so, Xenophon was not alone in feeling the benefits of being liberated from the sphere of Athens, even of Greece. His contemporary, Plato, also went outside the bounds of convention to invent the Philosopher King. Another contemporary, Isocrates, presented his finest portrait of the best leader in the figure of Evagoras, a famous king of the Cyprians. Though Xenophon is often seen as conservative or traditional in so much of his thinking, his Cyrus hardly

---

[2] Cf. Herodotus *Histories* 1.30–32. Consistent with the Solonic model, Cyrus is comfortable in his wealth, performs patriotic service with remarkable deeds, and sees his sons survive him. But scholars have wondered whether he leaves behind an untarnished legacy like Tellus, Cleobis, and Biton.

[3] See Hertlein 1886:vii–viii on the ancient tradition of reading the *Cyropaedia* in this way.

[4] Cf. Lenfant 200–209 and Llewellyn-Jones 2010:48–55. Xenophon's contemporary and fellow student of Socrates, Antisthenes, also wrote two works on Cyrus.

fits that description. Xenophon's idealization of ancient Persian life may have been whetted by his own (failed) mercenary campaign to replace Artaxerxes II with Cyrus the Younger (d. 401 BCE) on the Persian throne. Cyrus' achievement of establishing the Persian Empire itself plays into one of the central features of Xenophon's Theory of Leadership,[5] namely, the leader's ability to summon "willing obedience" from his followers.[6] Cyrus' achievement of empire was a historical fact. For Xenophon it seems to have been improbable that this vast number of diverse peoples, at least the majority of them and at least for a time, would not have been "willing participants" in the new, grand enterprise. He would not have been the last person in human history to imagine that there was something intrinsically harmonious about an empire.

For all the simplicity of the narrative and the foreignness of its subject, the *Education of Cyrus* has over long periods of time captured the interest of many leaders and students of leadership: Plato, Scipio Africanus, Cicero, Machiavelli, Thomas Jefferson, Leo Strauss. This present study will not focus on the reception of Cyrus except to the extent that some of the views of those who have read the *Education of Cyrus* still influence contemporary discourse on it. James Tatum's *Xenophon's Imperial Fiction* remains an important source for how the *Cyropaedia* was received in Europe for centuries. Paul Rasmussen's recent work, *Excellence Unleashed: Machiavelli's Critique of Xenophon and the Moral Foundation of Politics* (2009), reminds scholars of the ancient world that Xenophon's Cyrus is still central to discussions of contemporary political theory. A new (loose) translation of the *Cyropaedia* by Larry Hedrick illustrates the abiding relevance of Cyrus to anyone interested in leadership studies, whether in business, the military, or politics.[7]

Literary, Historical, and Theoretical Questions

Over the past three decades scholars have found the *Education of Cyrus* to be a fruitful source of fascinating questions. Tuplin, in his introduction to *Xenophon and his World*, observed over a decade ago:

> No part of Xenophon's *oeuvre* has seen such a change in its status as an object of serious study in the last generation as *Cyropaedia*—no doubt because so many of the general trends which have drawn attention to

---

[5] In referring to Xenophon's "Theory of Leadership" I am borrowing a term from Wood 1964 and Gray 2011:7, but it needs to be clarified since Xenophon has not always been seen as a theoretical thinker in the same sense as Aristotle, for example. I explain below (pp. 6–7) what I mean by this term.

[6] Cf. Gray 2007:7–8.

[7] For Cyrus as a model for the modern military leader, see Pease 1934.

Xenophon combine in this particular text. Those who have taken the trouble to look have discovered that what was apt to be seen as an over-long and over-bland piece of historical fiction actually has consider-able subtleties.[8]

Some of these perceived subtleties have been literary. Into what genre should the *Cyropaedia* be categorized? Is it a biography, a novel (romance), a history, or philosophy? Is Xenophon forging a new genre? If so, is he doing it in conscious distinction from other genres or just fashioning it to suit the occasion? Is he borrowing narrative material and narrative techniques from traditional Persian story-telling? What is Xenophon trying to accomplish by writing the *Cyropaedia*? Is it to instruct others on the art of leadership? Is it a call for such a leader as Cyrus to emerge in Greece? Is it to make a subtle case for a Greek inva-sion of seemingly decadent Persia, just as Xenophon's contemporary, Isocrates, had done explicitly?[9] Moreover, how does the *Cyropaedia* relate to Xenophon's other literary works? In particular, where in the *Cyropaedia* is Socrates? Is he Cyrus' father, Cambyses, who engages in a lengthy "Socratic" dialogue with his son and, like Socrates, expands his son's notions of what counts as good lead-ership? Does Socrates fill the role of the unfortunate sophist who is executed after the Armenian king becomes jealous of his son's affection for him? Is Cyrus himself "Socratic"?

Other questions about the work may be classified as historical. There is general scholarly consensus that in composing the *Cyropaedia*, Xenophon did not intend to write history, at least in two respects. First, his narrative is devoid of many names, geographical locations, and chronological sequences (annalistic or otherwise) that would have been readily available to him. It is also possible that Xenophon fabricated some of his characters, such as Cyaxares, the Medan uncle of Cyrus, who serves as a well-meaning foil and sometime blocking figure to Cyrus' ambitions.[10] Second, though Xenophon claims to be presenting a Cyrus that he has discovered *through investigation* (cf. 1.1.6), he does not present variant accounts of Cyrus' career (though he was certainly aware of them). Also, he neither weighs the probability of one version against another, nor defends the account he has given us as "true." He does not even give the impression that he has omitted any irrelevant aspects of Cyrus' life in favor of the more inter-esting ones.

---

[8]   Tuplin 2004:20.
[9]   Cf. Carlier 1978:336: "It is legitimate to search in the *Cyropaedia* for elements of answers to ques-tions that the Greeks were often asking around 360 BC: is the conquest of Asia possible? Is it sustainable? What will be the political repercussions? What will become of the Greeks who leave, and of those who stay?"
[10]   Cf. Tatum 1989:115–133, Gera 1993:106–109.

Yet, this is far from saying that the *Cyropaedia* is entirely fictional. Cyrus was a historical figure, and Xenophon clearly borrows events from his career that agree with other sources. We are thus left with an abundance of interesting questions. What is Persian about the *Cyropaedia* and what is Greek or "Xenophontic"? What were Xenophon's sources and how did he use them to construct his own Cyrus? Did he go beyond Herodotus and Ctesias to other authors of *Persica*? To what extent did Xenophon have access to Persian oral tradition, perhaps on his campaign with the 10,000 mercenaries in the *Anabasis*?[11] Part of what makes these questions so interesting is that for every facet of the *Cyropaedia* that feels familiarly "Greek," there are many that do not.

For example, the Persian educational system (*agôgê*) under which all elite Persians were raised according to Xenophon, has long reminded scholars of the similar system in Classical Sparta. It is strict, highly militaristic, and segregated (young boys train away from their homes). Yet the Persian education, more ethically focused, is not as severe as the Spartan one (cf. Xenophon *Constitution of the Lacedaemonians* 2). It is distinct from the Athenian education in that Persians go to school to learn moral virtue, Xenophon says, just as Athenians go to school to learn their alphabet.

According to Herodotus, the Persians actually have their own system of education. In this system, they train their youth to do three things: use a bow, ride a horse, and speak the truth (*Histories* 1.136). Cyrus the Younger receives just this sort of education, as Xenophon describes it in the *Anabasis*. Finally, the virtues that Persians learn are virtues that Xenophon regularly extolls as proper to the character of a gentleman and a leader. The Persian education in the *Cyropaedia*, then, is probably better thought of as a composite of the Spartan one, the Persian one (as well as Xenophon could recreate from his sources), and an idealized system created according to what Xenophon himself had deemed important.

In general, whenever we encounter any facet of the *Cyropaedia*, it is helpful to consider its Persian, Greek, Greek historiographical, and Xenophontic (and fourth-century Athenian) contexts. Sometimes all these contexts may tell us the same thing. For example, probably the Persians, Greeks, Greek historians, and certainly Xenophon thought that good horsemanship was part of good leadership.[12] In other cases, these contexts may not agree, and we may have a better insight into the source for Xenophon's perspective.

---

[11] See Sancisi-Weerdenburg 1985 for a discussion on the possibility of such sources and what may be preserved through oral tradition.

[12] Briant 1996:19–20 argues that despite Xenophon's claim that the Persians learned to ride horses because Cyrus introduced the practice from the Medes, their conquests under him seem to have necessitated a well-established equestrian culture.

Aside from literary and historical questions, which are often crucial to other questions, by far the most abiding questions about the *Cyropaedia* have been ones about Xenophon's so-called "Theory of Leadership" and the character of the central figure of the work, Cyrus. An associated and almost unavoidable question has been that of Xenophon's own political leanings. Is he democratic, oligarchic, monarchic, imperialist, or anti-imperialist? Before proceeding further with the history of this debate, it is important to pause for a moment and say, generally, what I mean when I say that Xenophon had a "Theory of Leadership." It will be clear from the examples I use below that I believe that Gray (2011) and I are using the term in a similar way, but let me say what I mean by it.

Xenophon does not ever use the term "theory" in his works. He seldom uses terms that could be translated as "leadership" or "leader," although he does speak regularly of the art of kingship. In fact, the types of leader he discusses (king, general, philosopher, estate manager) tend to have a monarchical bent, however collaborative and democratic the roles may be at times. Xenophon and his characters (with the exception of Socrates) do not typically seek definitions of the terms they use nor do they create a technical vocabulary for discussing theoretical topics, practices we commonly see in Aristotle and sometimes in Plato. Xenophon never defines the three main terms that will be the focus of this study (*philanthrôpia*, *philomatheia*, and *philotîmia*), though he does give a lengthy description of *philanthrôpia* in the *Cyropaedia*. Thus, when we speak of his "theory," what scholars generally mean (and what I mean) is that Xenophon talks about leadership across several different fields (e.g. domestic, military, political) and he seeks features common to each (see the discussion of Gray below, p. 11). He and his characters ask general questions about leadership. He praises leaders, criticizes them, and shows them to be somewhere between praise and criticism. Many of his works are centrally "about" leadership (e.g. the *Hieron*, *Agesilaus*, *Anabasis*, *Cyropaedia*, *Oeconomicus*, and arguably the *Memorabilia* and *Hellenica*). He talks about leadership in terms of lessons or *mathêmata* (from Socrates, Cyrus, Cyrus' father, Cambyses, Ischomachus, Xenophon himself) that are then put into practice and illustrated in narrative form. Part of this study will be engaged in asking the question, how *good* a theorist is Xenophon? In other words, does he give lessons in leadership that are fundamental (as opposed to traditional or simply practical) and comprehensive? (We would expect both features from Aristotle's theories on metaphysics, ethics, or politics.) In the end, this question may be the same as asking whether Xenophon is a theorist at all. In these several ways, I believe it makes more sense to say that Xenophon is more of a theorist than, say, Homer, Pindar, or Herodotus, all of whom feature leaders and their traits. At the same time, we do not have to conclude that Xenophon is as self-consciously theoretical as Aristotle.

One of the specific fundamental questions that seems to apply to all forms of leadership and that scholars have typically asked of Xenophon's Cyrus is to what extent does the leader reconcile his or her own needs and interests (e.g. for luxury, glory, wealth, power, privilege, safety, friendship, sex, romance) with those of the followers? Some scholars have argued that Cyrus does *not* achieve this reconciliation because several of his friends and followers are manipulated or marginalized in his selfish pursuit of empire (if it is even accurate to say that he is *pursuing* an empire).[13] A recent work by Gray, *Xenophon's Mirror of Princes* (2011), has formally divided the approaches to Cyrus' leadership into two distinct camps. First are those who take a more straightforward, face-value view that Xenophon meant to present Cyrus as a great leader, worthy of emulation, just as he was perceived by the Roman general, Scipio Africanus, for example. Others (e.g. Strauss, Tatum, Nadon), whom Gray identifies as having a darker, more pessimistic interpretation of Cyrus, see Xenophon's leader as at times manipulative, overly ambitious, and even ruthless.[14] It is here that Cyrus has been seen as more Machiavellian. In its extreme form this view assumes that any attempt to see the career of Cyrus in a positive or virtuous light must necessarily be naïve, conservative, or unintelligent.[15] Gray's sustained disputation of these pessimistic interpretations is the most thorough and multifaceted to date. I address this question further in Chapter One (pp. 33–44).

The Problems with "Ideal" and "Utopia"

While Gray's dichotomy may somewhat oversimplify a broad range of views on Cyrus, it is helpful in clarifying the traditional lines of a debate that has sometimes corresponded to different disciplines. Classicists are more often in the

---

[13] Though it seems likelier that he has in mind the Cyrus of Herodotus or Ctesias, Plutarch groups Cyrus, Alexander, and Julius Caesar together as three conquerors who had an "inexorable lust for empire and a mad desire to be first and best" (ἔρως ἀπαρηγόρητος ἀρχῆς καὶ περιμανὴς ἐπιθυμία τοῦ πρῶτον εἶναι καὶ μέγιστον, *Life of Antony* 6.3.3). At one point in his campaign against the Assyrians, Xenophon's Cyrus sends for reinforcements from Persia on the assumption that the Persians would desire an empire (*archê*) in Asia and the revenues from it (*Cyropaedia* 4.5.14). Once Cyrus has acquired his empire, he refers to this generic action as a "great achievement" (7.5.76). Cf. Ambler 2001:11–18 for a survey of the various ways in which Xenophon's Cyrus has been seen as entirely self-interested in this ambition and ultimately corrupt and corrupting.

[14] Dorion 2010 characterizes well the intellectual underpinnings of such an approach.

[15] Cf. Rasmussen 2009:xvi–xvii or Reisert 2009:296–297, who asserts that Cyrus' "ruthless and unscrupulous methods" have been "amply and persuasively documented." As is customary in such debates, at issue is what it means to be a "careful reader": political scientists find fault with those who, after 2,500 years of western political science, are not sufficiently skeptical or cynical of a character's political motives, while Classicists complain that non-Classicists are ignorant of the nuances of language as well as the literary and historical milieu in which Xenophon worked.

"straightforward" camp and political scientists in the "ironic" camp. I would like to take an additional step here in clarifying this debate before I move to the main questions about Cyrus' leadership that will be the focus of this work. Two terms tend to pervade criticism of the *Cyropaedia*: we often hear that Cyrus is Xenophon's "ideal" leader and that the empire he comes to govern is a "utopia."[16] Despite their origin in the Greek language, neither "ideal" nor "utopia" has an obvious ancient Greek equivalent, at least not in the Xenophontic lexicon.[17] This is not to say that that we can never use words that Xenophon himself never used to critique his work (I am in fact assuming he has a "Theory of Leadership"), but in this case both of these terms can be misleading and are not very helpful as long as they have connotations of perfection, completeness, immutability, or otherworldliness, like the Platonic Forms. Calling Cyrus "ideal" also increases the possibility that we will see any less than perfect portrayal as ironic or subversive.

But there is no great subtlety to the fact that Cyrus is *not* an "ideal" leader. Cyrus is for Xenophon a historical figure with mortal limitations, and Xenophon inherited a literary tradition that saw him as such. For example, in his youth Cyrus envies the cupbearer, Sacas, who enjoys privileged access to his grandfather. He rushes impulsively into the hunt and almost gets himself killed. Later he glories over the sight of dead bodies killed in a raid against the Assyrians. His grandfather, Astyages, who is otherwise full of fondness, is disappointed in him. Elsewhere Cyrus admits to feeling vulnerable to erotic desire, greed, and pride, all of which he tries to combat with careful forethought. It is fair to say, however, that Xenophon's portrait of Cyrus is stripped of the more critical aspects we encounter in other authors (e.g. Herodotus, Ctesias, Isocrates, Plato). Herodotus is aware of other accounts of the career of Cyrus but neglects to include them in his *Histories*, perhaps because they were flattering beyond credibility. Thus we might say that Xenophon's portrait is "idealized" or "embellished," but Xenophon's Cyrus is (I think, obviously) not an "ideal" leader. The most that may be said accurately, according to Xenophon's own language, is that Cyrus was "best" in a number of virtuous qualities and likely offered to Xenophon's audience as an example for emulation. From this vantage we may then ask if

---

[16] This tendency dates as far back as Cicero, who calls Xenophon's Cyrus a "model of proper command" (cf. *effigiem iusti imperii*, *Letters to Quintus* 1.1.23), and Dionysius of Halicarnassus, who call him the "likeness" of a good and happy king (cf. εἰκόνα, *Letter to Gnaeus Pompeius*, 4.1.7). The *Cyropaedia* has even been called a "utopian" work (cf. Stadter 1991b), which is an appropriate term, properly understood, to describe literature but is not very helpful in describing the Persian Empire at the time of Cyrus' death in Book Eight.

[17] On the problems with, and pervasiveness of, the concept of utopia in discussions of fourth-century Greek thought, see Dillery 1995:42–54.

Xenophon ever does anything to undermine his Cyrus, while bearing in mind that to show Cyrus as less than ideal should not count as undermining him.

Similarly, Cyrus does not govern a utopia. Babylon, the former seat of the Assyrian empire, is portrayed by Xenophon as complex and most hostile. Despite some efforts at offering equal freedoms and honors to the members of many nations, Cyrus' own Persia stands in privileged distinction over the rest. Xenophon even says in his preface that Cyrus ruled others *by fear*. We should not try to paper over this fact any more than Xenophon does, for it is not a subtle or ironic point. We can try to understand, however, the degrees to which "rule by fear" may not have seemed as troublesome to Xenophon as it does to us. In Book Three, the Armenian prince Tigranes argues that fear of Cyrus taught the Armenian king to feel self-restraint and obedience toward him. These feelings eventually translate into a mutually beneficial alliance. Another indication that Xenophon may have had different standards for the leader's treatment of the conquered enemy than we do is his account of the Spartan king Agesilaus (*Agesilaus* 1.28). Agesilaus sold captive barbarians into slavery, naked, so that his men would see how fat, lazy, and effeminate they had become and thus have the courage to fight them. Yet, this leader was also celebrated for his habitual kindness to a vanquished enemy. That Xenophon could be subverting his encomium for a dead Spartan king by pointing out his cruelty seems highly unlikely.[18]

Xenophon could have portrayed Cyrus seamlessly winning over *all* nations with grace and skill. Instead, it seems that he was interested in showing Cyrus navigating more treacherous waters, adapting his leadership style to accommodate the changing necessities of the moment. As Breebaart has said:

> Xenophon's 'superior system' is a calculated attempt to direct human psychological realities to superior ends. The foundations of obedience being compulsion, self-interest and rational organization, the 'system' actually consists in a complex of 'ways and means' to manipulate people to a better understanding of self-interest. In the *Hiero*, too, the reformed tyrant will achieve to be accepted and respected by the citizens, when he succeeds in convincing them of the virtual identity of their own interests with that of the ruler.[19]

---

[18] Chapter Four treats the employment of eunuchs, another of Cyrus' practices that might seem to involve cruelty (and thus Xenophon's subversion of an "ideal" leader).

[19] Breebaart 1983:130n44. I stipulate in Chapter One that there is an additional foundation to obedience as Xenophon sees it in the example of Cyrus, namely, his ability to take empathetic pleasure in the good fortune of his followers, which they in turn appreciate and reciprocate. The leader-follower relationship is not merely predicated on an exchange of goods and services as Breebaart suggests.

Finally, the decline of the Persian Empire after Cyrus, often considered a strike against his leadership, need not be seen as such. Persian decline was a widespread assumption among Greeks both before and during Xenophon's time. Thanks to Herodotus (or Plato), Greeks could see all nations necessarily experiencing similar fluctuations over time.[20] That no government, even the best one, is stable for very long is a claim Xenophon makes in the very first sentence of the *Cyropaedia* (perhaps because he is reading Herodotus). Cyrus himself stipulates that the maintenance of an empire is not automatic, but requires the greatest attention (7.5.76). As many scholars have noted, Xenophon sees the same decline in Sparta in his *Constitution of the Lacedaemonians*.[21] Dillery reminds us of another perspective on Persian decline: in the *Hellenica* Xenophon saw his own Greece in decline and also an opportunity to save it by a campaign against a declining Persia.[22] Moreover, the emergence of decadent leaders after the death of a great ruler was a storyline pursued by Thucydides in the example of Pericles (*Histories* 2.65.10–11). Thucydides seems to want to emphasize the greatness of Pericles rather than any failure of his to train better replacements or establish more permanent institutions. I discuss Cyrus' role in Persian decline further in Chapter Four (pp. 88–89).

How Good a Leadership Theorist is Xenophon? Comprehensiveness and Fundamentality

With "ideal" and "utopia" either removed from the discourse, or carefully qualified, we may begin to see areas where scholars can discover more common ground from which to discuss Cyrus. Thus, rather than begin from the assumption that Xenophon's Cyrus' is ideal or idealized, I would like to suggest one more particular approach: let us identify certain problems of leadership, familiar to Xenophon, his predecessors, and contemporaries and try to determine the thoroughness with which Xenophon addresses them. Our basic question, then, will be "Is Xenophon's Theory of Leadership a good one?" I don't necessarily mean "good" in an absolute sense, in the way that the leadership theorist Peter Drucker seems to mean when he calls the *Cyropaedia* "still the best book on leadership."[23] I mean "good" in the sense of whether or not the Theory addresses the numerous problems of leadership recognized in the vast

---

[20] For the accuracy of the notion that Persia was in decline in Xenophon's time, and the general question of how prevalent the view was among Athenians that Persians were decadent, cf. Sancisi-Weerdenburg 1987 and Miller 1997, respectively.

[21] Cf. Dillery 1995:192.

[22] Dillery 1995:20.

[23] See Hedrick 2006.

ancient Greek literature on governance, especially Xenophon's fourth-century Athenian contemporaries (e.g. Plato and Isocrates). One earlier example of such an approach is Azoulay's discussion of Cyrus' use of ceremony and luxury (*truphê*). He shows how Cyrus strikes a careful balance between the more austere Persian and more lavish Medan customs.

We may wonder further: Is Xenophon's Theory of Leadership "hierarchical"? Does it have a foundation followed by derivative aspects? Obviously one difficulty of this approach is that, whether or not Xenophon's Theory of Leadership meets this criterion, he doesn't present his theory in anything like a straightforward philosophical treatise with technical terms and careful distinctions, or even a sustained philosophical dialogue like Plato's *Republic*. Instead, we must comb through shorter dialogues, historical narratives, sympotic dramatizations, or, in the case of the *Cyropaedia*, an extended quasi-biography.

Again, Gray's recent work provides a very helpful account of many aspects of Xenophon's Theory of Leadership from all these sources, which we will summarize here.[24] According to Xenophon, leaders are distinct from followers, and one of the main distinguishing characteristics arises from the leader's superior self-control. The goal of leadership is defined as the success of the followers, a success that may take the form of material prosperity, security, or moral improvement. Leaders lead primarily by winning the willing obedience of the followers, which they obtain by having greater knowledge as well as other virtues. The ability to win this obedience is itself teachable. Thus the leader, whether a general, a king, or an estate manager, may help women and slaves learn to lead others. Finally—and this is where Xenophon's views may be described as truly "theoretical"—leaders are similar in all fields: they instruct, reward or punish, guard the land, toil, and strive to win willing followers.

Many aspects of Xenophon's Theory of Leadership may be found in other ancient authors, as Gray notes. Plato also treats the "willing obedience" of the followers in the form of what we might call "political" self-restraint (*sôphrosunê*), the condition that obtains in a state where all members agree on who should lead and who should follow (*Republic* 432a). The followers will not necessarily understand the leader's goals for the state; in fact they may even need "noble lies" to help them reach this condition of political *sôphrosunê* (*Republic* 414c–415c).[25] Plato's Socrates also opens up leadership to women. Although slaves are not mentioned explicitly, they are given implicit access by the principle that justice in a city requires that everyone perform a role according to his or her nature.

---

[24] Gray 2011:7–24.

[25] For the implications of the noble lie for leadership and good government, cf. Reeve 1988:208–213.

Isocrates defines success for the group in similar terms as Xenophon (i.e. protection, prosperity, moral edification), both in his encomium to Evagoras and his speech to Nicocles. Evagoras, he says, transformed his citizens from barbarians to Hellenes, made them civilized and gentle, and protected them from the Persians (*Evagoras* 66–68). Nicocles learns that kings must relieve their states from distress, guard their prosperity, and render them great from being small (*To Nicocles* 13). Xenophon, Plato, and Isocrates all consider self-restraint to be paramount. Isocrates even has Nicocles proclaim that his self-restraint is so great that he has neither sired children by anyone one but his wife (in order to keep his lineage pure) nor had sexual relations with anyone outside of marriage (*Nicocles* 36–42).

For all of the important things that have been said about Xenophon's Theory of Leadership thus far, scholars have not made a sustained attempt to understand the character of the leader in fundamental terms.[26] Perhaps the most obvious reason for this is that Xenophon is still considered less a theoretical thinker than a conscientious preserver of traditional Greek views about leadership. Yet, given his large body of work, we should ask of him what leadership traits, if any, make up a necessary and sufficient set. If self-control is one of them, then we may ask what other traits does self-control *allow* or *cause* a leader to have. If self-control is not fundamental, does Xenophon ever explain or show what more basic trait is conducive to it?

The Love of Wisdom as Fundamental to Plato's Theory of Leadership

In assessing these features of Xenophon's Theory of Leadership as it pertains to character, we may take a cue from Plato and his portrait of the Philosopher King. In the *Republic*, Socrates explains that a love of wisdom (*philosophia*) is the foundation of good leadership, conducive to the four so-called Classical virtues of wisdom (*sophia*), justice (*dikaiosunê*), courage (*aretê*), and self-restraint (*sôphrosunê*).[27] For Socrates, wisdom is the knowledge of an otherworldly reality made up of Forms that are "ideal" in the sense of "perfect," "unchanging," "undying," and "complete," whether the Form be of a Square, a Table, Justice, or the Good. A person who is in love with such wisdom, and loves it to the exclusion of everything else, will have no concern for the body or the perceptual

---

[26] The traits of leadership that are the focus of this work, *philanthrôpia*, *philomatheia*, and *philotîmia*, are treated by Due 1989:163–170, 181–183 and cursorily by other authors, but not with the level of attention that is warranted for Xenophon's Theory of Leadership to be understood.

[27] The following summary of the explanation for the fundamentality of the love of wisdom is taken from *Republic* 485d–487a.

world unless they facilitate an understanding of this other world of the Forms. Accordingly, such a person would be just, insofar as he or she would have no interest in cheating or harming others for the purpose of material gain.[28] Such a person would also have courage because there would be no reason to fear death, which is seen as a reunion with the realm of the Forms. Finally, such a person would have true self-restraint, not merely momentary self-restraint in hopes of greater pleasure. The pleasures of the body (food, drink, sex, sleep) and the emotions (fear, pity, anger, lust) could not distract the *philosophos* from focusing on the pursuit of true wisdom.

Does Xenophon provide us with a Theory of Leadership that is merely a collection of positive and negative traits he has observed over time? Or does he integrate and prioritize them in the same way Plato does with the Philosopher King? For example, we noted that Xenophon praises self-restraint as a trait that distinguishes the leader from the follower, but how does a leader come by it? Surely a Theory of Leadership ought to try to answer this question. Moreover, it was thought in the ancient world that Xenophon's *Cyropaedia* was conceived of as a criticism of the *Republic*. Aulus Gellius explains that there was a perceived tension between Plato and Xenophon: neither mentions the other in any of his works, their portrayals of Socrates differ in terms of their fields of interest, and Plato makes disparaging mention of Cyrus in the *Laws*.[29] Diogenes Laertius also perceived a rivalry between the two for the title of "first pupil of Socrates" (3.24). Whether there was an actual rivalry or not, there is abundant parallelism in their works. Both wrote dialogues of Socrates, both wrote *Symposia* and *Apologies* for Socrates, and Plato wrote the *Laws* and Xenophon the *Constitution of the Lacedaemonians*. Is the *Cyropaedia* somehow the counterpart to the *Republic*, at least as a theoretical work on leadership? Does Xenophon's Cyrus solve problems of leadership differently than Plato, whether in conscious distinction from him or not?

---

[28] Note that for Plato in the *Republic* political justice is "doing one's part" for the good of the *polis* according to nature (433a). It primarily entails not harming or cheating others, but does not necessarily entail caring about the well-being of other individuals so much as the overall well-being of the *polis*. I argue that for Xenophon justice does seem to involve concern for the well-being of others, evinced in the form of delight in their good fortune and grief in their suffering (pp. 64–66).

[29] This perceived tension is described in the second-century CE work, the *Attic Nights* (14.3). Gellius does not believe that the evidence proves that there was a tension so much as similarity of talents that converged on the same questions and material. The tension derives, he says, from their respective fans. Cf. Hirsch 1985:97–100. Danzig 2003 argues that Plato responds to the *Cyropaedia* in the *Laws* but not in a way that takes Xenophon's portrayal of Cyrus very seriously. He does point out that the *Cyropaedia* and *Laws* are similar in some respects, especially in that they both show greater concern (than the *Republic*) for how a good political regime might actually be instituted (295–297).

These questions have two initial answers that invite us to explore Xenophon's Theory of Leadership more deeply. First, Xenophon says in the *Cyropaedia* that Cyrus was "most loving of being honored" (*philotîmotatos*)—*in his soul*.[30] He does not stop there. He asserts that this love of honor resulted in two other key leadership traits, a love of risk-taking (*philokindunia*) and a love of toil (*philoponia*).[31] We will have occasion to explore these traits further, but for now we note that Xenophon has made an attempt to organize leadership traits according to the fundamental (*philotîmia*) and the derivative (*philokindunia*, *philoponia*), just as Plato makes *philosophia* fundamental and *sôphrosunê* derivative from it.

Secondly, Cyrus' extraordinary love of honor may solve a fundamental problem of leadership. As we noted above, one of the fundamental (we might say "universal") problems of governance is how the leader, who by general consensus must work for the happiness of the followers, manages to reconcile their interests with his or her own desire for wealth, power, privilege, security, luxury—whatever. For, despite Socrates' assertion that a physician is still a physician whether you pay him or not (*Republic* 342d), the leader needs some motivation to engage in leadership, since it is a role that generally involves greater toil, greater mental effort, greater responsibility, and many more dire consequences in the event of failure than the role of follower. Plato admits that the Philosopher King will not want to lead for the sake of leading; he or she would rather study philosophy than engage in the mundane practices of running what is ultimately an imperfect state. Plato instead proposes to get the Philosopher King to lead by one of two means. Either the community will forcibly compel the Philosopher King to lead; or it will remind the King of his obligation to them for raising him in an enlightened environment, and he, being a just person, will presumably acquiesce (347b–c, 519c–520d). Xenophon, by contrast, solves this problem much more simply, if imperfectly. Cyrus' love of being honored (*philotîmia*) compels him to undergo all the risks and toil required of a leader. Honor (*tîmê*) is at least a large part of his motivation to lead; it is how he seems to reconcile his interests with his followers, honor for leadership service.

---

[30]   *Cyropaedia* 1.2.1.8. It can be misleading to translate *philotîmia* as "the love of honor" because this may imply that the lover of honor has a desire to do what is objectively moral or good. Yet the term quite often emphasizes the desire for the *subjective* recognition of the person dispensing the honor (though the Greeks certainly recognized the difference between the honor that a good person bestowed and that of a bad person). As Xenophon himself uses it here, "the love of being honored," effectively means "the desire to win praise from others," which he elsewhere calls the sweetest pleasure (*Hieron* 1.14, *Memorabilia* 2.1.31). On *philotîmia* in ancient Greek society, see Whitehead 1983 and Dover 1974:230–233.

[31]   Cf. also *Cyropaedia* 1.5.12.

So, here we have two leads in pursuing further questions about Xenophon's Theory of Leadership. First, to what extent does Xenophon prioritize traits of leadership and, second, how well, in the end, do these qualities address the various nuances to the problems of leadership as Xenophon and his contemporaries saw them? More specifically, we may ask how well Xenophon's description of *philotîmia* meets the many criticisms that Plato makes of it in the *Republic*.

Now that we have lighted upon the mention of Cyrus' *philotîmia*, it is helpful to explore the larger context of the passage it appears in, Xenophon's summary statement on Cyrus' soul:

φῦναι δὲ ὁ Κῦρος λέγεται καὶ ᾄδεται ἔτι καὶ νῦν ὑπὸ τῶν βαρβάρων εἶδος μὲν κάλλιστος, ψυχὴν δὲ <u>φιλανθρωπότατος</u> καὶ <u>φιλομαθέστατος</u> καὶ <u>φιλοτιμότατος</u>, ὥστε πάντα μὲν πόνον ἀνατλῆναι, πάντα δὲ κίνδυν ον ὑπομεῖναι τοῦ ἐπαινεῖσθαι ἕνεκα.

In his nature Cyrus is reputed and still celebrated even now among the barbarians as most beautiful in his form and *most loving of humanity* in his soul, as well as *most loving of learning* and *most loving of being honored*, to the point that he would endure every labor and undergo every danger in order to be praised.

Cyropaedia 1.2.1

This is a tripartite, alliterative, and superlative formulation of Cyrus' character traits. Here, again keeping Plato in the back of our minds, we may wonder how much this parsing of Cyrus' soul is meant to contrast with Plato's appetitive, spirited, and rational parts of the soul (*Republic* 435c–441c). Is this Xenophon's "thesis statement" capturing what he felt was the character of all good leaders?[32] Does this account for other important leadership traits, in that they may be derived from it? These are the central questions we have set out to answer in the present study.

Other Summary Statements of Excellent Leadership

Xenophon's summary of Cyrus' nature is the only one of its kind (succinct, tripartite, superlative, alliterative), though other formulations have some of its features. As early as Homer's *Odyssey*, we observe Odysseus' succinct formula for

---

[32] To my knowledge Azoulay 2004b:321 (in his treatment of Cyrus' *philanthrôpia*) is the first to suggest that Xenophon's summary statement on Cyrus somehow captures the essence of his entire character.

a perfect king. Disguised as a beggar, he begins his conversation with his wife Penelope by likening her fame to that of such a leader:

> O lady, none of the mortals on the boundless earth could criticize you. For truly your glory reaches the wide heaven, like that of a blameless (*amumôn*) king who, being pious (*theodeês*), lords over many valiant men and upholds justice (*eudikia*), and the black earth produces wheat and barley, and trees are heavy with fruit, and the flocks give birth to sure offspring, and the sea brings forth fish as a result of his good leadership (*euêgesia*), and the people thrive under him.
>
> *Odyssey* 19.107–114

In the *Anabasis*, Xenophon praises Cyrus the Younger as the most kingly and most worthy to rule since Cyrus the Great. According to Xenophon, Cyrus was best in everything as a young boy in the Persian education system:

> Here, then, Cyrus was reputed to be, in the first place, the most modest of his fellows (*aidêmonestatos*), and even more obedient to his elders than were his inferiors in rank; secondly the most devoted to horses (*philippotatos*) and the most skillful in managing horses; he was also adjudged the most eager to learn (*philomathestatos*) and the most diligent (*meletêrotatos*) in practicing military accomplishments, alike in the use of the bow and of the javelin. Then, when he was of suitable age, he was the fondest of hunting (*philothêrotatos*) and, more than that, the fondest of incurring danger (*philokindûnotatotos*) in his pursuit of wild animals.
>
> *Anabasis* 1.9

Later in the *Anabasis*, Xenophon provides three contrasting leadership portraits: the war-loving Clearchus, the great-souled Proxenus, and the lover of wealth, Menon (2.6.1–29). How consistent are these portrayals of the best leadership with that of Cyrus in the *Cyropaedia*? Does Xenophon's work, late in life, represent the culmination of his clearest and most succinct formulation of the best kind of leadership, or it is something of a deviation from previous notions?

In his encomium to Evagoras, a work thought to have inspired Xenophon's encomium to Agesilaus, Isocrates portrays the Cyprian king as boy with beauty (*kallos*), strength (*rhômê*), and self-restraint (*sôphrosunê*), who augmented these traits in adulthood with courage (*andria*), wisdom (*sophia*), and justice (*dikaiosunê*) (*Evagoras* 22–23). He praises the 14-year old Alexander the Great for his reputation as a lover of humanity (*philanthrôpos*), a lover of the Athenians (*philathênaios*), and a lover of wisdom (*philosophos*) (*To Alexander* 2). To Timotheus of Heracleia, he laments that Timotheus' father, Clearchus, had once been most liberal (*eleutheriotatos*), most gentle (*praôtatos*), and most loving of humanity (*philanthrôpotatos*) but after attaining tyrannical power became the opposite (*To Timotheus* 12). He praises the Cyprian Demonicus' father for being a lover of beauty (*philokalos*), magnificent in his appearance (*megaloprepês*), and generous (*koinos*) toward friends (*To Demonicus* 9). Curiously, it is not until the first century CE with Athenagoras' praise of the Roman emperor Marcus Aurelius that we again see the coupling of the superlative love of humanity and learning that we see in Xenophon's Cyrus (2.1.6).

The Importance of the Leader's Nature and Education over Birth and Fate

In describing Cyrus as most "philanthropic," most loving of learning, and most loving of honor, it is debatable whether Xenophon is referring to Cyrus as an adult or as a child. He may be describing character traits formed in the course of Cyrus' life by education and experience.[33] Yet, the fact that Cyrus exhibits these traits even in his youth suggests that Xenophon means to present them as innate, even if they are honed and enhanced over time (cf. 1.3.3., 1.4.1, 1.4.3.).

Another reason we should focus on Xenophon's portrayal of Cyrus' character is that it seems to be the primary explanation for Cyrus' success. Xenophon does not seem very interested in Cyrus' lineage. By contrast, this facet of leadership *is* played up by the historical Cyrus on the Cylinder Seal and then by Darius on the Behistun inscription. In his introduction, Xenophon points out that Cyrus was the son of the Persian king Cambyses and Mandane, daughter of the Medan king Astyages (1.2.1). He makes no attempt to connect Cyrus' nature to theirs, however.[34] Cyrus does receive an education of sorts from both his father and grandfather, but neither education highlights any hereditary similarity. Cambyses instructs Cyrus in the same dialogue form, with much of the same content, that Socrates uses with young men in the *Memorabilia*, but none of this instruction reflects any heredity link between father and son. Xenophon is not retelling the story of Odysseus and Telemachus.[35] Moreover, the education that Cyrus receives from his grandfather is of a negative kind; despite his affection for

---

[33] Cf. Due 1989:147–152.

[34] The Lydian King Croesus does attribute Cyrus' success to his divine and regal lineage as well as his lifelong practice of virtue (*Cyropaedia* 7.2.24). The Mede Artabazus justifies his devotion to Cyrus, in part, because he regards Cyrus as descended from the gods (4.1.24).

[35] Cf. Gera 1993:50–72.

Astyages, Cyrus seeks to avoid his excesses of food and drink, as well as his extra-legal kingship (*Cyropaedia* 1.3.4–18). At the end of the *Cyropaedia*, Xenophon seems equally uninterested in connecting Cyrus to his degenerate sons (8.8.2, 8.7.23). By contrast, he focuses much more on the lineage of the Spartan king, Agesilaus, the other most celebrated leader in his writings (*Agesilaus* 1.2–5). In this instance, Xenophon favors his contemporary, Isocrates, and the later biographer Plutarch, who do find ancestral traits, both physical and ethical, in their subjects.[36]

Xenophon also seems relatively uninterested in Cyrus' fate or destiny, whereas his fate is foretold in so many examples in Herodotus and Ctesias. Cyrus is the agent of divinity in the Hebrew and Babylonian traditions as well. In the Book of Ezra, he is roused by Yaweh to build a temple in Jerusalem (Ezra i.1–5). In the Book of Isaiah he is "the anointed one" (Isa xlv 1). On the Cyrus Cylinder, he is the agent of the god Marduk, sent to restore peace to Babylon after the cruel reign of Nabonidus.

Thus, of the three modes of explanation for Cyrus' success as a leader (nature, lineage, fate), Xenophon focuses almost entirely on the first. But, unlike his lineage and fate, Cyrus' education is an important part of his character. We should not assume that the traits that make what Xenophon thought of as Cyrus' nature or his soul could not have been enhanced by education. Nevertheless, education is not the complete picture. Other Persian youths will have had the same training as Cyrus, seemingly for generations, as Xenophon explains when he summarizes this institution (1.2.2–16). In the *Memorabilia*, Socrates observes that even when men have been raised under the same customs and laws, they have naturally different degrees of courage arising from different degrees of inherent daring (*Memorabilia* 3.9.1–2). I am thus interested in what Xenophon finds so special about Cyrus' nature, what qualities enable him to establish the Persian Empire.

The Structure of This Inquiry

As we proceed with our attempt to understand Cyrus' three superlative traits of leadership, we will be using five different, though not always distinct, contexts. These contexts are necessary for understanding not only the *meaning* of these traits, but also their *import*. In order to know whether Xenophon is being "light" or "dark" in his portrayal of Cyrus, it is important to keep in mind the writer's

---

[36] The practice of characterizing children in terms of their parents is often found in Homer. The epinician poet Pindar does it as well, always mentioning the father, and often his exploits, when he praises the victory of a son. In his treatment of Agesilaus' lineage, Xenophon may be following the model of Isocrates' *Evagoras* (cf. Marchant 1925:xviii–xx), in which Isocrates links the king's traits to those of his mythological ancestors, the Aeacidae (*Evagoras* 13–18).

experiences, the authors he was reading, the cultural climate in which he wrote, and the points of comparison or contrast he may be explicitly or implicitly drawing. Accordingly, first, we have Xenophon's own writings, all of which have come down to us. And Xenophon seems to have had fairly consistent views about leadership across his entire corpus, sometimes at the level of repeated examples and phrases. Secondly, we have what we could call the "Greek literary tradition," authors like Homer, Pindar, and Thucydides, who have many things to say about good and bad leadership and who were a known influence on Xenophon. Third, within the Greek literary tradition we have contemporaries of Xenophon, especially Plato, Isocrates, and Demosthenes, who were Athenian authors with abundant things to say about what traits made the best leaders. Fourth, we have historians like Herodotus and Ctesias, who are known to have been Xenophon's sources for the content of Cyrus' life. In the case of Ctesias, the information is fragmentary and in summary form and thus always in need of delicate interpretation. Finally, we have original Persian material that Xenophon may have been privy to, either in the form of inscriptions or oral tradition.[37] In some cases, there are formal elements of Persian literature, like "the king's dying speech," that may have been adapted by Xenophon to conform to his own objectives.

It is not always possible to trace the exact source of a Xenophontic influence because of the scarcity of material. What's more, in the case of Socrates, we cannot determine whether Xenophon was *influenced* by the "real" Socrates or whether Xenophon's Socrates is the *product* of Xenophon's own views. In the end, we cannot hope to have arrived at a full description of Xenophon's Theory of Leadership, but our attempt will be to move further in the direction of a theory as it pertains to character.

In addition to these contexts, while I mean to include all relevant evidence from the entire *Cyropaedia*, I will be focusing heavily throughout on the following specific scenes, as they have emerged in the course of study as the best sources for answering the questions I have posed. In Book One, Cyrus reveals a lot about his three superlative traits when he spends part of his youth in Media with his grandfather and boys of his own age. He regales his family at lavish banquets with his precociousness and learns to excel in horsemanship and hunting (1.4). Later in Book One, Cyrus engages in a lengthy dialogue with his Persian father, Cambyses, in preparation for the campaign against the Assyrians that will take up most of the work. Here Cyrus learns the finer points of leadership but also exhibits his own budding wisdom (1.6). In Book Three, Cyrus pursues and

---

[37] Xenophon says that Cyrus is celebrated and remembered by the Persians to have had the kind of soul that he describes (cf. διαμνημονεύεται, 1.2.2.2). Strabo (15.3.18) claims that Persians had a custom of remembering the deeds of their gods and noblest men in song. Cf. Mueller-Goldingen 1995:67n14 on this claim.

then captures a rebel Armenian army. He puts the Armenian king on trial, but gently listens to a defense from his son, Tigranes. He ultimately pardons the king and turns him into a devoted ally. In this same scene, Cyrus also makes Tigranes pardon his father for executing (out of envy) the sophist that had been Tigranes' teacher as a boy (3.1). After his success in forming this alliance and several others (including winning over many Medes), Cyrus himself becomes a source of envy for his uncle, Cyaxares, now king of the Medes. In their confrontation, Cyrus disarms Cyaxares and effectively "leads his leader" by a careful blend of forcefulness and obedience (5.5). In the course of his pursuit of the Assyrians and their wicked king, Cyrus defeats Croesus, king of the Lydians, and engages in a lengthy dialogue (reminiscent of their encounter in Herodotus) on the nature of the good life, the folly of flattery, and the importance of knowing oneself (7.2). Finally, in Book Eight, Cyrus adapts his leadership style to introduce an imperial court in Babylon, including an elaborate administration (especially the Persian satrapies), imperial pomp, and a system of education designed to make others adopt the virtues that Cyrus himself had learned in the Persian educational system.

In the following chapters, we will explore as carefully as we can what Xenophon means by Cyrus' *philanthrôpia, philomatheia,* and *philotîmia.* This investigation will comprise the bulk of Chapters One and Two. In Chapter Three, we will tackle the question of how good a leadership theorist Xenophon is by trying to determine the extent to which these three character traits form the *foundation* of other leadership qualities, or share some close relation to them. Finally, in Chapters Four, Five, and Six, we will test the *comprehensiveness* of these three leadership traits against the more or less obvious problems of governance that someone with these characteristics is likely to face. We will draw these problems from Xenophon's contemporaries as well as from earlier Greek literature and even from other versions of the Cyrus legend. It is my hope that these problems, though not completely solved by Xenophon, will be of interest to students of ancient or modern theories of leadership, as well as those interested in how cross-cultural interaction can lead to the production of Xenophon's Theory of Leadership.[38] This work is thus meant to study the "foundations" of Xenophon's Theory of Leadership in two senses, cultural and conceptual.

---

[38] Modern leadership theory has sought to reduce leadership to a set of finite traits that are necessary and sufficient for "good" leadership (cf. Gardener 1990, Goethals 2006). One of the implicit arguments of this book is that Xenophon should be at the center of any of these discussions. Anyone familiar with the widely popular work of Kouses and Posner, for example, may read this book (or the works of Xenophon) to see how many leadership practices were already anticipated in the fourth century BCE.

1

Philanthrôpia and *Philotîmia* as Reciprocal Fondness

I BEGIN THIS STUDY of Cyrus' three superlative character traits with an early and seemingly simple passage in the *Cyropaedia*. Xenophon describes how the twelve-year-old Cyrus wins over his Medan contemporaries (*hêlikotai*), then their fathers, and then his grandfather, Astyages. Both the love of humanity (*philanthrôpia*) and the love of being honored (*philotîmia*) explain Cyrus' behavior. As we proceed through this passage piece by piece, we will see how thoroughly interwoven Xenophon's entire narrative is and how he is either reworking or incorporating aspects of the Cyrus legend from Herodotus and Ctesias.[1] It is also possible that Xenophon is either inventing aspects of Cyrus on his own or that he is drawing from non-extant Persian folklore. Of particular interest for us will be the ways in which Cyrus comes to form intimate relationships. We will examine his fondness for others, his affection, his ways of showing favor, his gentleness, his sense of fairness, his sympathy, his pity, his nurturing attention, his ability to play "matchmaker," his practice of giving gifts—all of which serve to win honor and a devoted following.

The scene is set by the departure of Cyrus' mother, Mandane, from the Medan court of Astyages back to Persia. After expressing concern for the kind of education Cyrus would receive in a decadent and despotic Media, she leaves Cyrus behind. He must rely on his own Persian education, which is tested in several ways. Xenophon describes how Cyrus quickly comes to be on familiar terms with his Medan contemporaries and disarms their fathers. He then wins over Astyages and uses his favor to help the fathers.

ταχὺ μὲν τοῖς ἡλικιώταις <u>συνεκέκρατο</u> ὥστε <u>οἰκείως διακεῖσθαι</u>, ταχὺ δὲ τοὺς πατέρας αὐτῶν ἀνήρτητο, <u>προσιὼν</u> καὶ ἔνδηλος ὢν ὅτι <u>ἠσπάζετο</u> αὐτῶν τοὺς υἱεῖς, ὥστε εἴ τι τοῦ βασιλέως δέοιντο, τοὺς

---

[1] Since my primary focus is on Cyrus' leadership, I do not make generalizations about Xenophon's reworking of Herodotus and Ctesias, but I suggest where I believe this reworking may occur.

παῖδας ἐκέλευον τοῦ Κύρου δεῖσθαι διαπράξασθαι σφίσιν, ὁ δὲ Κῦρος, ὅ τι δέοιντο αὐτοῦ οἱ παῖδες, διὰ τὴν <u>φιλανθρωπίαν</u> καὶ <u>φιλοτιμίαν</u> περὶ παντὸς ἐποιεῖτο διαπράττεσθαι, καὶ ὁ Ἀστυάγης δὲ ὅ τι δέοιτο αὐτοῦ ὁ Κῦρος οὐδὲν ἐδύνατο ἀντέχειν μὴ οὐ χαρίζεσθαι. καὶ γὰρ ἀσθενήσαντος αὐτοῦ οὐδέποτε ἀπέλειπε τὸν πάππον οὐδὲ κλαίων ποτὲ ἐπαύετο, ἀλλὰ δῆλος ἦν πᾶσιν ὅτι ὑπερεφοβεῖτο μή οἱ ὁ πάππος ἀποθάνῃ· καὶ γὰρ ἐκ νυκτὸς εἴ τινος δέοιτο Ἀστυάγης, πρῶτος ᾐσθάνετο Κῦρος καὶ πάντων ἀοκνότατα ἀνεπήδα ὑπηρετήσων ὅ τι οἴοιτο χαριεῖσθαι, ὥστε παντάπασιν ἀνεκτήσατο τὸν Ἀστυάγην.

Quickly he had *blended in* with his age-mates so much that *they were like family.* Quickly he won over their fathers *by approaching them* and making it clear that he *favored* their sons; the result was that if they needed anything from the king, they would tell their sons to ask Cyrus to accomplish it for them. And Cyrus, *because of his* <u>philanthrôpia</u> *and* <u>philotîmia</u>, made it a priority to accomplish whatever they asked of him. And Astyages could not resist favoring Cyrus in whatever he asked for. For when he was sick, Cyrus never left his grandfather and never stopped weeping, but made it clear to everyone that he feared his grandfather might die. For if Astyages needed something even at night, Cyrus was first to notice it and with the least hesitation of all would jump up to help in whatever way he thought would be pleasing, so that he won over Astyages entirely.

Cyropaedia 1.4.1–2

As we think about this scene, we should keep in mind how *Herodotus'* Cyrus interacts with his Medan contemporaries and their fathers (*Histories* 1.114–116). Herodotus' Cyrus is ten years old and, up to this point, raised in the company of herdsmen who have rescued him from exposure (he does not yet know of his royal blood). He plays at being "king" with the Medan youth, but when it is his turn to be king he assigns various tasks, then has one of the boys whipped for refusing to obey. As the boy is seemingly of a higher station than Cyrus, the boy's father, Artembares, has Cyrus brought before Astyages to be punished for his outrage. Astyages then realizes that Cyrus is the grandson he had tried to have killed as an infant (because he feared his rise to power). Both Xenophon and Herodotus' Cyrus play at being king but in rather different ways. Xenophon's Cyrus imagines being ruler (*archôn*) of Astyages' wine-pourer Sacas, but in a lighthearted and ultimately harmless manner (*Cyropaedia 1.3.11*).

Blending In

Unlike Herodotus' Cyrus, Xenophon says that Cyrus "blended in" so well with his Medan contemporaries that he comes to be on "familiar terms" with them. Other uses of the expression *oikeiôs diakeisthai* refer to those whose interests and routines are thoroughly intertwined, e.g. by dining together, traveling together, or sharing in any activity with a member of a household (*oikos*) without technically belonging to it.[2] Cyrus is especially good at forming these kinds of relationships. When he is introduced to his grandfather, he kisses him as one "naturally loving of affection" (*philostorgos*), as though Astyages were a long-lost friend (1.3.2). Though literally a son, grandson, and nephew, Cyrus assumes the role of family member to others. He is the avenging "son" to the Assyrians, Gobryas and Gatadas.[3] Cyrus plays the "brother" to Abradatas by protecting and caring for his wife Pantheia (6.4.7.5). Ultimately he is a "father" to the citizens of his many nations, and they are his children.[4] Cyrus shows sympathy for Croesus by emphasizing their common humanity.[5] He also wins over the wine-pourer Sacas by becoming "his own Sacas," by which Xenophon means that, in enlisting the cupbearer's guidance, Cyrus develops an intuitive sense for when to visit his grandfather (1.4.6). This friendship between Cyrus and Sacas may be a reworking of Ctesias' account of how the low-born Cyrus insinuates his way into the inner court of the Medan king by becoming his cupbearer.[6]

After mentioning his quick intimacy with the Medan youth, Xenophon gives specific examples of how Cyrus manages to "blend in" with them so well. He attributes none of Cyrus' familiarity to his half-Medan ancestry but instead portrays what in other contexts is called Cyrus' mildness or gentleness (*praotês*).[7] With false bravado Cyrus challenges his contemporaries to riding contests, even though he knows he is inferior. When he fails, he is quick to laugh at himself (1.4.4). When he goes hunting with his comrades, he declines the privilege of being the first to cast his spear, but insists instead that his comrades be allowed to hunt with him on equal terms (1.4.14). When the hunt begins, Cyrus even cheers his comrades in pursuit of their quarry. His grandfather delights in the

---

[2] Cf. Isocrates *Trapeziticus* 3.4–5, *To Philip* 20.3, Lysias 1.39.1, and Aeschines *Against Ctesiphon* 138.3.

[3] *Cyropaedia* 4.6.2.9, 5.2.7–8, 5.3.19.

[4] *Cyropaedia* 8.1.1, 8.1.44, 8.8.1. For Cyrus' subjects as "sons" or "brothers," cf. 8.6.16.

[5] *Cyropaedia* 7.2.10. On Cyrus' humane treatment of Croesus in Herodotus, see Lefèvre 1971: 403–404.

[6] Cook 1983:26 on Ctesias F8d*5–7. All fragments of Ctesias are taken from the edition of Llewellyn-Jones (2010).

[7] This trait, and its relation to *philanthrôpia*, is discussed in Chapter Three, pp. 66–69.

fact that Cyrus does not feel any envy toward them. Instead Cyrus is a source of pleasure to all and of grief to none (1.4.15).

Cyrus' friendly competitiveness contrasts sharply with the envy of the Assyrian king in the *Cyropaedia*, who not only murders the son of Gobryas when he bests him in the hunt, but makes Gadatas into a eunuch when he catches the eye of one of his concubines.[8] Cyrus' gentle competitiveness takes on even greater significance when we consider the context of Ctesias' *Persica*. During the reign of Artaxerxes I, Ctesias explains, Megabyzus was slated for execution for hunting a lion against the king's royal prerogative.[9] Xenophon's Cyrus apparently has no need for such a privilege.

Fortunately for his claims to royal sovereignty, Cyrus eventually surpasses his comrades in both horsemanship and hunting, but without marginalizing or humiliating them. He is in effect "playing king" all along, as in Herodotus, though without treating his comrades as disobedient slaves. Moreover, with the exception of his uncle, Cyaxares, Cyrus never comes to rival any of his comrades in a threatening or destructive way. Whereas Ctesias' Cyrus liberates the Persians *from* the Medes, who are portrayed as inferior and unworthy to rule,[10] Xenophon's Cyrus adapts to both cultures and eventually incorporates aspects of Medan society into his Persian Empire.

Showing Favor

After Xenophon says that Cyrus *quickly* wins over his Medan comrades, he says that he *quickly* wins over their fathers as well (1.4.1). He does this first by making an approach to their fathers, an act of some boldness (*tolmê*), given the reluctance that Cyrus later shows in approaching his own grandfather (cf. 1.4.13). Cyrus then makes clear to the fathers that he holds their sons in his favor. The verb, *aspazomai*, can mean to greet or welcome someone, often with a handshake. In Xenophon the verb is even more formalized. When Cyrus first meets his grandfather, he greets him (*aspazomai*) and Astyages greets him in turn (*antaspazomai*),[11] giving him a beautiful Medan cloak. Here Cyrus is formally recognized as part of the house of Astyages. In contrast, Herodotus' account has Astyages send Cyrus away immediately upon recognition, feigning affection (*Histories* 1.121). Later in Xenophon when Cyrus' uncle, Cyaxares, feels alienated

---

[8] *Cyropaedia* 4.6.4, 5.2.28. This is the second, unnamed, Assyrian king, son of the first king, who is killed by Cyrus' army. Historically, this king was Nabonidus (556–539 BCE).

[9] F14.43; cf. Llewellyn-Jones 2010:60.

[10] Cf. F8d*14–19.

[11] This is the first appearance of this term in extant Greek literature and is perhaps invented to capture a particular Persian mode of greeting.

from his Medan subjects, Cyrus encourages him to receive their greeting and return it (5.5.42). When Cyrus himself departs Media, he distributes gifts to his contemporaries, giving his Medan robe to one special friend as a sign that he holds him in highest favor.[12] Again, by showing his favor with a beautiful cloak, Cyrus emulates the kingly behavior of his grandfather.

"I Want You to Want Me"

As a consequence of the favor that Cyrus shows their sons, these Medan fathers enlist Cyrus to be an ambassador to Astyages. Cyrus, for his part, considers it a high priority to fulfill all their requests. Xenophon often gives manifold motivations for a character's actions; in this case Cyrus has two: *philanthrôpia* and *philotîmia*. It can be misleading to translate *philanthrôpia* as "love of humanity" since in English the phrase can suggest a feeling felt by a fortunate person of high status for the poor and downtrodden. In the context of Cyrus' affection, gentleness, concern for fairness, encouragement of others, and versatile ability "to blend in," his *philanthrôpia* seems to be more of a *fondness* for others and for sharing their company.[13] And while we could translate his *philotîmia* as "a love of being honored," the term seems to point more to Cyrus' affective desire for *popularity, approval,* or *acceptance* from his Medan contemporaries. Just as he is fond of them, he hopes to win their fondness in turn, to be *their* favorite.[14]

Later in Chapter Four, Cyrus' comrades play upon his desire for popularity in order to convince him to persuade his grandfather to let them go hunting in the wild. When they threaten to find someone else to ask Astyages, Cyrus is "stung" and summons the courage to do it himself (1.4.13). Elsewhere, Cyrus is portrayed striving to win gratitude from Cyaxares and Astyages (1.3.12). After a lengthy campaign, his Persian comrade Hystaspas gently teases him for wanting to rush home to be congratulated by his father (6.1.4–5). Thus, rather than wanting merely symbolic honors bestowed by a community (though he seems to want these, too), Cyrus seems to crave emotional approval and praise from the individuals he himself likes or respects. We recall that in his summary

---

[12] Cf. ἠσπάζετο, 1.4.26.5. There are several variations of the text here, which suggest that Cyrus either gave the robe to the one he favored most or gave the robe *to show* whom he favored most. I have used the reading in Bizos's edition.

[13] Cf. Dover 1974:201.

[14] Ctesias also presents Cyrus as someone who is able to win over others (though he does not explain how), particularly his mentor Artembares and Astyages himself, though this affection seems one-sided. Cyrus, in fact, manipulates Astyages' fondness for him in order to secure leave to plot the liberation of the Persians from the Medes.

statement of Cyrus' superlative soul, Xenophon says that his *philotîmia* translated specifically into a desire to be praised.[15]

By contrast, Ctesias' Cyrus, though certainly a lover of honor, pursues it in a less personal fashion. He forms one close friendship with the Persian Oebaras, who continually plies him with fantasies of winning glory among the Persians by liberating them from Media, even to the point of sacrificing other friends who are an obstacle to the overall mission (F8d*14–19). Yet, Cyrus' pursuit of glory takes place independently of a desire for the respect and approval of others. Though Astyages is not Cyrus' grandfather in Ctesias' version, he shows several signs of feeling affection for the young man (F8d*6–7, 22); he is not the murderously cruel or duplicitous Astyages we see in Herodotus. In fact he feels personally betrayed when Cyrus revolts:

> Alas! I resolved often enough not to treat bad men well, but I have been ensnared by fine words all the same: I took on Cyrus, a wicked goatherd, a Mard by birth, and produced such utter destruction for myself.
>
> Ctesias F8d*30

Moreover, Cyrus' father (Atradates in this version) does not command his son's respect. In fact, Atradates wins a pardon (and a proper burial) from Astyages for his part in the Persian rebellion on the grounds that Cyrus had been disobedient to him (F8d*37). Whereas in Xenophon Cyrus' father, Cambyses, is a mentor and dialectician on the level of Socrates, Cyrus' father in Ctesias is the unwitting dupe of his son's ambitions. In sum, Ctesias' Cyrus, in his pursuit of honor, does not show the reverence, gratitude, and obedience of Xenophon's Cyrus, who learns gratitude as part of his education.[16]

High Honors

Yet, although wanting acceptance, Xenophon's Cyrus sometimes keeps to his own standards of what honors he should pursue and accept, despite the commands and censure of others. As we noted above (p. 24), Cyrus shows some initiative in his approach to the fathers of his Medan friends. Xenophon says that he undertakes *all* labors and *all* risks to win praise; this principle seems to apply even to the point of disobedience.[17] We see this risk-taking in his first hunting expedition with his uncle, Cyaxares (also in 1.4). Here, Cyrus eagerly

---

[15] In the *Hieron*, Simonides calls praise the sweetest of all sounds. Hieron in turn distinguishes true praise from flattery, of which he says tyrants must always be suspicious (1.14–15).

[16] *Cyropaedia* 1.2.7, 1.4.25, 1.5.1, 1.6.20. Cyrus the Younger is "most obedient" (*Anabasis* 1.9.5).

[17] Cf. the similar relationship between the love of honor and risk-taking at *Memorabilia* 3.1.10.

learns all that he needs to know about which animals he may hunt and which he must avoid. Nevertheless, at the first sight of a deer, Cyrus gives chase and is almost thrown from his horse. He hits the deer with a spear and is subsequently chastised by his elders. Though he is vexed by the criticism, he still darts off in pursuit of a wild boar "like someone possessed" (*enthusiôn*); Cyrus' pursuit of honor is not altogether rational. Accordingly, Cyrus is again chastised by his uncle for his boldness (*thrasutês*). Yet, he begs for the opportunity to give the kill to his grandfather even if he is whipped for it. Cyaxares reluctantly relents, saying, "for you are now our *king*" (1.4.9). For his part, Astyages is grateful for Cyrus' gift but does not see that it was worth the risk. In his first battle with the Assyrians, Cyrus is victorious but also a source of concern because he becomes "mad with daring" (cf. τῇ τόλμῃ, 1.4.24.4). Here, all three Cyruses (Xenophon's, Ctesias', Herodotus') share a sense of extraordinarily daring ambition. In Herodotus, Cyrus is also willing to be punished for his treatment of Artembares' son because the son, after all, had disobeyed a "king" (1.115). In Ctesias, Cyrus is willing to risk even death to liberate the Persians.

Like the other two Cyruses, Xenophon's subject does not pursue just any honor, but the highest honor. He has a passion for work (cf. 1.4.5.5). He is willing to take risks and endure censure—even corporal punishment—to achieve this honor (1.4.13). He is, we could say, a great-souled man, *megalopsychos* (or *megalophrôn*), even though this term is uncommon in Xenophon.[18] Iscocrates says of Evagoras, king of Cyprus, in his encomium to him:

> We will find that humans who love to be honored and are *great-souled* (μεγαλοψύχους) not only prefer praise to lavish funeral services [which are proof only of wealth], but gladly choose to die rather than live, striving for a good reputation more than a livelihood and doing everything possible to leave behind an immortal memory of themselves.

> *Evagoras* 3

Isocrates reports that Evagoras' own great soul was enough to instill in the Persian king, Artaxerxes II, the fear that he might be overthrown (59). Plutarch reports that Alexander takes a mortal risk to tame the mighty Bucephalus and in doing so wins praise from his father, who says that he should "seek a kingdom greater than Macedonia" (*Life of Alexander* 6). Not only does Xenophon's Cyrus show a similar passion for horses, but he has an outsized appetite for hunting, quickly bringing down all the creatures in his grandfather's zoo and appealing for the opportunity to hunt all the animals in existence, as though they were

---

18 Aristotle (*Nicomachean Ethics* 1123b–1125a, *Eudemian Ethics* 1232a19–1233a30) has a fuller description of the great-souled, "small-souled," and vain man.

"bred for him" (*Cyropaedia* 1.4.5). Both Cyrus and Alexander are portrayed as young and future conquerors who pursue the highest honor by taking greater risks than those around them think prudent or necessary. This level of successful risk-taking forms the basis of their claim to greater sovereignty. Both flirt with kingship from a very young age.

Matchmaking

In addition to this desire for popularity through the pursuit of the highest honors, Cyrus' other path to sovereignty is paved with the favors he does for his friends. To return to the central passage of our discussion, Xenophon says that the Medan fathers used Cyrus to deliver petitions to Astyages. This facet of Cyrus' behavior is interesting for two reasons. First is what it reveals about Astyages' court: the fact that Cyrus is required to bring petitions from the Medan noble fathers implies a measure of distance between the king and his most prominent subjects. As Azoulay has shown, Cyrus' court eventually displays the right combination of both distance and intimacy between the leader and his followers, a Medan and Persian blend.[19] Second and more importantly, Cyrus' practice of serving as an ambassador becomes habitual. On three separate occasions, he reunites Tigranes, Abradatas, and Croesus with their captive wives.[20] He marries the daughter of Gobryas to the Persian Hystaspas and offers to find another wife for Chrysantas, calling himself an accomplice (*sunergos*) and expert at matching people (5.2.12, 8.4.13–22). Cyrus awards a music-girl to a Medan who is a "lover of music" (5.1.1). Guided by luck or fate, he even pairs the Persian commoner Pheraulas in lasting friendship with a Sacian horseman (8.3.26–50). Cyrus reconciles Tigranes with his father, the king of Armenia, after the king had killed Tigranes' mentor out of envy (3.1.38–40). He plays the peacemaker between Chaldaeans and Armenians by uniting them through intermarriage and land-sharing. Xenophon concludes his account of their treaty by noting that it continues to this day, underscoring the prudent nature of Cyrus' arrangement.[21] He says that Cyrus received from the people throughout his empire whatever they had in excess and then returned to them whatever they needed (8.6.23).

Xenophon also points to two instances where Cyrus *tries* to be a match-maker. The young Cyrus approves when a larger Persian boy steals a larger coat

---

[19] Azoulay 2004a:168–169.
[20] *Cyropaedia* 3.1.36–37, 6.4.7–9, 7.2.26–28.
[21] *Cyropaedia* 3.2.17–24. Cyrus is the indirect peace-maker for the Carians in their civil war (7.4.1–6). Cf. Gera 1993:281. Cyrus the Younger reconciles Clearchus, Menon, and Proxenus (*Anabasis* 1.5.15–17).

from a smaller boy and gives the boy his own (smaller) coat.[22] On his deathbed, Cyrus attempts, unsuccessfully, to reconcile his two sons for a harmonious transition of power.[23]

The political advantages of Cyrus' successful pairings are obvious, and Xenophon typically makes them explicit. When Cyrus mounts a campaign against the Assyrians, many Medes follow him because of the service he had done for them in their youth on behalf of their fathers *out of* philanthrôpia (4.2.10.8–9). In return for Cyrus' protection of Pantheia, Abradatas gives his life in service to Cyrus' army. In the union between Gobryas' daughter and Hystaspas, the Persian and Assyrian nations are also united. In all of these scenes, Cyrus is instrumental in establishing strong romantic or friendly bonds that, in other contexts, he will take pains to weaken (as I discuss below, p. 33).

The ability of a leader to forge these kinds of alliances is nothing new to human history,[24] but it has a certain Xenophontic or perhaps Socratean flavor. In Xenophon's *Symposium*, each guest is challenged to tell which skill he is most proud of. Socrates, for his part, answers ironically that he is most proud of his skill as a pimp (*mastropeia*), explaining that the practitioner of this art beautifies the woman he is to match to her client (3.10). The higher form of this art is practiced by Antisthenes, whom Socrates dubs a "go-between" (*proagôgos*) for pairing people according to their interests (4.61). Such a skill, Socrates says, has grand social and political significance:

> The man who recognizes beneficial partners and can make them desire one another would, it seems to me, be able to make cities into friends and to forge useful marriages, and would be very valuable for cities and citizens to have as a friend or an ally.
>
> Xenophon *Symposium* 4.64.3–8

Xenophon notes in the *Memorabilia* that Socrates not only taught others as much as he knew, but also introduced them to those with greater expertise.[25] In an erotic context, Socrates so effectively plays the "pimp" for the courtesan Theodote by telling her how her beauty can capture rich men that she jokingly asks him to be her "co-hunter" (*Memorabilia* 3.11.15).

---

[22] *Cyropaedia* 1.3.17. The significance of Cyrus' approval of this transaction, and his misapplication of justice, is discussed further below (pp. 64–65).

[23] *Cyropaedia* 8.7.13–18. Cf. Gera 1993:122–123.

[24] In the Hebrew tradition, for example, Yaweh plays the matchmaker (Cf. Midrash Rabbah, Genesis 68:3–4).

[25] *Memorabilia* 4.7.1. Cambyses gives the same advice to Cyrus (*Cyropaedia* 1.6.14) and Cyrus tells his sons to learn from history if they cannot learn from him (8.7.24). On the theme of multiple sources of education, see Gray 2011:19–20.

Attentive Care

Both Socrates and Cyrus are adept at pairing the interests of others. In order to secure favors for the fathers of his Medan contemporaries, however, Cyrus works another aspect of *philanthrôpia* with his grandfather and does it so well that Astyages cannot resist any request from him. Xenophon says that Cyrus surpasses all others in tending to Astyages' needs when he is sick and in showing his sympathy by weeping constantly for him. By contrast, Ctesias' Cyrus uses the *pretense* of being an attentive healer, not to Astyages but to his own father. By claiming to want to nurse his father back to health, Cyrus plays on Astyages' affection to secure leave from his court so that he may plot an attack on the Medes and liberate the Persians (F8d*22).

In Xenophon, however, Cambyses advises the young Cyrus to express sympathy and show attentive or "hands on" care (*therapeia*) to his followers, which he does on numerous occasions. In Book Eight, as part of a long list of "philanthropic" activities, Xenophon explains that before Cyrus is able to benefit others materially, he does his best to show that he takes "pleasure in their good fortune" (recall Cyrus cheering his comrades in the hunt) and that he "felt bad for their misfortune."[26] Again, Cyrus contrasts sharply with the Assyrian king, who does not show any remorse or sympathy for Gobryas after he had killed his son (*Cyropaedia* 4.6.5).

Cyrus, for all his self-mastery, is also the most lachrymose character in Xenophon's works, at least statistically. Fifteen of twenty-six references to tears or shedding tears occur in the *Cyropaedia* and five refer to Cyrus (i.e. when he leaves the Medes as a boy, when he sympathizes with Cyaxares' frustration over losing the affection of his own soldiers, and when he witnesses the suicide of Pantheia and the funeral of Abradatas).[27] Only five other characters in Xenophon feel pity (*eleos*) and none in more than one instance, making Cyrus also the most compassionate character. In fact, all instances of Cyrus' pity are for non-Persians and extend to several different nations: Gadatas (an Assyrian), the Egyptians, and the Lydians, Pantheia and Croesus.[28]

---

[26] Cf. τῷ συνηδόμενος μὲν ἐπὶ τοῖς ἀγαθοῖς φανερὸς εἶναι, συναχθόμενος δ' ἐπὶ τοῖς κακοῖς, 8.2.2–3. Cf. also 1.6.24. In an instance of Xenophon's highly-selective diction, these are two of only three places where he pairs the verbs for sharing in the suffering of others (*sunaxthomai*) and sharing in their joys (*sunêdomai*), the other being in his discussion of mutual love in the *Symposium* (8.18). Elsewhere in Xenophon Socrates advises the courtesan Theodote to share in the success and suffering of her lovers (*Memorabilia* 3.11.10.6–8), and Ischomachus recommends the sharing of sympathies and interests as a way of securing the loyalty of a maidservant (*Oeconomicus* 9.12).

[27] *Cyropaedia* 1.4.26.2, 1.4.28.15, 5.5.10.3, 7.3.8.2, 7.3.11.2.

[28] Cf. *Cyropaedia* 5.4.32, 7.1.41, 6.1.47, 7.3.14, 7.2.26. Other instances of pity include the elder Assyrian King's pity for Gobryas over the loss of his son (*Cyropaedia* 4.6.5.7). Cleander pities the wounded

As part of his expressions of *therapeia*, Cyrus visits the injured Gadatas, who marvels that Cyrus should care for him without any obligation to do so (5.4.10–11). In the same battle-scene, a "clearly distressed" Cyrus tends to the wounded Cadusians so diligently that he skips dinner either to look after them in person or to send someone to care for them (5.4.17). On another occasion at a dinner, Cyrus notices the bandages of his wounded soldiers and asks about the cause (2.3.19–20). In pursuit of the Assyrians, Cyrus captures some of the Chaldaeans but has their shackles removed and orders surgeons to tend to their wounds (3.2.12.4). Cyrus wins over the Chaldaeans in much the same way as Xenophon's other great king, Agesilaus:

> Understanding that while a country that had been plundered and depopulated could not support an army for a long time but that one that was inhabited and cultivated could offer everlasting sustenance, he [Agesilaus] prepared not only to master the enemy with force but also to reconcile them with gentleness. Often he told his soldiers not to punish prisoners of war as wrong-doers but to guard over them as human beings. Often, whenever he changed camp, if he saw the children of merchants left behind ... he took care that they be brought along, too. He ordered that those prisoners left behind because of old age be taken care of lest they be mangled by dogs and wolves. The result was that not only did those who learned about these things come to have good will for him, but even the prisoners themselves. And whatever cities he reconciled he removed from them the services that slaves perform for their masters and ordered them to obey in whatever ways freemen obey their leaders. And by *philanthrôpia* he gained control of fortresses that could not be taken by force.
>
> *Agesilaus* 1.20–22

As king of Babylon, Cyrus gathers the best physicians, equipment, and supplies at his palace. When someone is sick and requires attention, Cyrus watches over him and provides whatever he needs, not failing to show gratitude to the physicians (8.2.24–25). He even challenges his closest followers to compete with him in *therapeia* toward others (8.2.13–14). In performing the role of physician, Cyrus

---

soldiers under Cyrus the Younger (*Anabasis* 3.1.19). Xenophon pities himself and his comrades after they have been abandoned in enemy territory (*Anabasis* 3.1.19.2). Socrates and Antisthenes pity those who cannot live within their means (*Oeconomicus* 2.2.4, 2.7.4, 2.9.4, *Symposium* 4.37.2), though Simonides says this condition is not pitiable (*Hieron* 4.10.2). Other instances of pity involve unnamed subjects, self-pity, or claims that something is pitiable (*Anabasis* 1.4.8.1, *Oeconomicus* 7.40.4, *Apology* 4.4, *Memorabilia* 2.6.21, *Hieron* 1.37.1).

conforms to the education he receives from his father, Cambyses, who insists that a leader must ensure that his followers do not become sick at all.[29]

Cyrus' attentive care is similar to other "philanthropic" characters in Greek literature. Aristophanes in Plato's *Symposium* describes Eros as the "most philanthropic" of gods for being a physician to the ills brought on by erotic love (189d1). Pindar describes the divine centaur Cheiron as a wild creature "with a mind that is loving of men," whose love is expressed through his tutelage of the physician Asclepius, himself celebrated as a *philanthrôpos* in the fifth and fourth century.[30]

In other versions of Cyrus' rise to prominence in the Medan court, Cyrus is Astyages' official cup-bearer or his gardener, but in Xenophon it is by his *therapeia* that Cyrus works his way into his grandfather's favor.[31] Nor does he overcome the Medes by domination and conquest but by winning over his contemporaries with his generosity and winning over their fathers with his favor toward their sons. In every case, his behavior is dually motivated by a fondness for others (*philanthrôpia*) and a desire for *their* fondness (*philotîmia*).

Gift-giving

We have looked at several ways in which Cyrus expresses his fondness for others and wins them over, for example by being gentle, encouraging, sympathetic, and attentive. Yet, we have only taken a cursory glance at perhaps the most obvious method: giving gifts. This, too, is a practice Cyrus partakes of in his youth and develops over time. At the table of Astyages, Cyrus portions out pieces of meat to various servants as tokens of gratitude (1.3.7). Such a gesture also has the effect of winning distinction for Cyrus because it displays his capacity for self-mastery over food and drink (*enkrateia*). There is evidence to suggest that the practice of distributing food was common among Persian kings as a thoughtful way of compensating the servant staff.[32] Xenophon may be casting the young Cyrus as the inventor of this practice. Interestingly, Xenophon also advocates a similar practice in his dialogue between Simonides and the tyrant Hieron (*Hieron*). After Hieron has complained of the financial burden of main-

[29] *Cyropaedia* 1.6.16. On the leader-as-physician metaphor, cf. Patroclus (*Iliad* 11.837–848) and Alexander the Great (Plutarch *Life of Alexander* 8). On Xenophon himself as a physician and father, cf. *Anabasis* 5.8.1; Anderson 1974:122–123.

[30] Cf. νόον ἔχοντ' ἀνδρῶν φίλον, *Pythian Odes* 3.5. See Gera 1993:50 and Ferguson 1958:109.

[31] Cf. Drews 1974:389–390 on the version of Cyrus as a court gardener in Nicolaus of Damascus. In correspondence with me, Claire Taylor has made the plausible suggestion that Cyrus' *therapeia* and the servant-like role he plays to others may be carried over and modified from Ctesias' Cyrus, who is both a slave and then a servant.

[32] See Lenfant 2007:207 on a fragment of Heracleides of Cumae (F2) about the Persian king's dinner. This fragment argues against the belief that Persian banquets were lavish because of decadence.

taining a standing army, Simonides points out to him that it is less expensive for a monarch to give friendly greetings and to dole out prizes: "Don't you see how in horse races and gymnastic and choral competitions small prizes produce great expenditure, many labors, and many cares in humans?" (*Hieron* 9.11). Here it seems that Cyrus is engaging in a practice that has precedence in a Greek understanding of Persian history as well as in Xenophon's own opinions on how to practice efficient leadership through thoughtful gift-giving.

As a general practice, Cyrus allows servants to take food on an expedition and leads the servants to water like beasts of burden, both highlighting his generosity and reinforcing their servant status.[33] On the eve of the attack on Sardis, Cyrus performs a sacrifice, from which he continually gives meats "to the one most in need" (7.1.1.5). As a commander, Cyrus orders a generous meal to be prepared for the Medes and Hyrcanians when they return from pursuing the enemy on horseback (4.2.37–41; cf. 4.5.1). Once Cyrus has the wealth to transform his *philanthrôpia* into material benefaction, he excels at sharing fine food and giving thoughtful and lavish gifts (cf. ἡ πολυδωρία, 8.2.8.1). He hires the finest chefs, serving his guests the same food that he himself eats and assigning them honorific positions at the table.[34]

These practices not only have the predictable effect of winning honor for Cyrus but also the less obvious effect of minimizing the extent to which others may plot against him. Xenophon explains that Cyrus practiced *philanthrôpia* as a way of winning the good will of his followers but also of improving his own security (8.1.48–8.2.1). Because they were so thoughtful and so unique to the king, Cyrus' gifts rendered his followers more loyal to him than they were even to their own families (8.2.9). We see now that for Xenophon *philanthrôpia* does not have an *absolute* form of expression: sometimes it may involve bringing his followers closer together by matching their interests (e.g. reuniting Abradatas, Tigranes, and Croesus with their wives) or keeping them apart. What matters is whether the gesture brings honor (and security) to Cyrus.

Loving Humanity as a Means or an End?

Now that we have touched upon numerous instances where Cyrus' love of honor and love of humanity are carefully intertwined, we should consider if there are any ways to disentangle them. Scholars have long been bothered by this connection.[35] It can be worrisome to see Cyrus doing so much to win honor, and we

---

[33] *Cyropaedia* 8.1.43–44. For the view that Cyrus uses *all* gift-giving to enslave his honor-loving followers, see Reisert 2009.

[34] Cyrus the Younger uses banqueting in a similar way (*Anabasis* 1.9.26–28).

[35] Cf. Azoulay 2004b:323n229, Gray 2011:5–69 *et passim*, and Danzig (forthcoming):7–9.

would perhaps prefer a more "selfless" leader who leads either exclusively out of a love for fellow human beings or, like Plato's Philosopher King, out of a passion for conceptualizing the perfect state in conformity with the idea of the Good. Xenophon's Cyrus does not seem to share this preference. The question, then, is: *is Cyrus' love of humanity subordinate to his love of being honored, i.e. a means to an end?* Scholars have attempted to answer this question by pointing to places where Cyrus seems to use trickery or manipulation of his followers to his own advantage; showing *philanthrôpia* could be just such a trick. Coupled with this criticism is a more general criticism of Cyrus' apparent ambition for empire. Yet the fact that Xenophon attributes distinct motives, *philanthrôpia* and *philotîmia*, to Cyrus in the passage we considered at the outset of this chapter would suggest that he sees Cyrus exhibiting his love of humanity *for its own sake*. Fortunately, there are other places in the *Cyropaedia* we may look to in order to settle this question.

To clarify our understanding of this question further, we may consider four examples on the extreme end of "helping others for their own sake" that do not seem to fit exactly with Cyrus' expressions of *philanthrôpia*. First, Cyrus does not seem to have a "maternal instinct" toward his fellow humans or even his closest friends. Note Socrates' description of the mother:

> The woman conceives and bears the child, weighted down, at risk to her own life, and supplying her own food, with which she herself is nourished. And having overcome this great labor, she gives birth, raises the child and watches over it. *She has received no benefit nor does the baby know by whom it has been benefited* nor can it point out what it needs, but she herself guesses what will be beneficial and delightful and tries to supply them, and she raises the child for a long time, enduring toil both day and night, *knowing not what gratitude from these efforts she will receive.*
>
> *Memorabilia* 2.2.5

Even though he is a "father" to many, it seems there is nothing that would qualify as self-sacrifice in Cyrus. More common, we might say, is what Danzig calls a "coexistence of self-interest with a genuine concern for the good of others."[36] A good illustration of this coexistence is spelled out by Cyrus himself when he exhorts his comrades to help the eunuch Gadatas on the grounds that both sides will benefit (*Cyropaedia* 5.3.31).

Nor does Cyrus seem to exhibit quite the helping behavior of Jason, leader of the Argonauts and also an aspiring king. On one famous occasion Jason

---

[36] Danzig (forthcoming):8.

encounters Hera disguised as an old woman at the flood of the River Anaurus. Hera explains why she helps him win the Golden Fleece:

> Jason became greatly beloved by me, ever since he met me by the streams of the flooding Anaurus, when I was testing men's righteousness, and he was returning from the hunt. All the mountains and high peaks were being sprinkled with snow, and down from them torrents were tumbling in crashing cascades. And in my disguise as an old woman *he took pity on me and lifting me onto his own shoulders proceeded to carry me through the rushing water.* That is why he is ceaselessly held in highest honor by me.[37]

> Apollonius *Argonautica* 3.66–74, translation Race

Here Jason takes pity on an old woman and helps her cross the flooding river, apparently at some risk to himself. Cyrus, by contrast, is seldom shown risking himself for the unfortunate or those of a lower class, unless it is a gesture of gratitude, whereby he hopes to ensure their future services. Instead he competes to help his uncle, Cyaxares, and his grandfather, Astyages, the two most powerful men in Media, and feels especial delight in winning their favor (1.3.12). The closest comparison between his and Jason's behavior is in Cyrus' treatment of Pantheia after she commits suicide over the body of her husband, Abradatas, though this treatment involves no personal risk. Cyrus pities Pantheia, sheds copious tears, and honors both her and her husband with a lavish funeral (7.3.15–16). In fact, the Greek words describing Jason's feeling for Hera and Cyrus' for Pantheia are similar (cf. ὀλοφύρατο, κατολοφυράμενος). We could imagine that Cyrus honors Pantheia for his own political advantage; perhaps he wanted a reputation as someone who took care of his friends. Xenophon does not make any effort to suggest this, however. His Cyrus sheds real tears.

For all the comparisons that scholars have found between the two, Cyrus is also different from Xenophon's Socrates.[38] To defend him against the charge of corrupting the youth of Athens, Xenophon calls Socrates "philanthropic" and "caring toward the people" (*dêmotikos*) because he shared his wisdom *for free*

---

[37] A further testament of Jason's unflinching concern for others is the enthusiasm with which he hopes the blind seer Phineus may regain his sight (Apollonius *Argonautica* 2.438–442). Jason's enthusiasm may be characterized as non-self-interested because by this point in the epic he has already received all of Phineus' prophetic insight.

[38] Due 1989:198–203, Gera 1993:26–131, and Rasmussen 2009:81–97 trace the influence of Socrates on the *Cyropaedia*, though none compare their *philanthrôpia*. As Gera 1993:27 notes, it is difficult to determine whether Xenophon's Cyrus derives from Xenophon's understanding of the historical Socrates or his opinions about leadership influence his portrayal of both figures. Cf. also Higgins 1977:56 on Cyrus' and Socrates' incorporation of erotic language to characterize their roles as leaders.

and always improved those around him.[39] Socrates' *philanthrôpia*, he argues, was even more extraordinary than conventional benefaction:

> Socrates brought distinction to the city in the eyes of the rest of the humanity *much more than Lichas*, who was famous for his service to Sparta. For Lichas used to entertain guests in Sparta who were attending the gymnastic festivals, but Socrates, for his entire life, used to lavish the greatest of his gifts upon whoever wanted them. For when he sent his associates away he had made them better.[40]
>
> *Memorabilia* 1.2.61

Like Socrates, Cyrus' *philanthrôpia* does not seem motivated by a love of material gain; in fact, he goes to great lengths to pass up the wealth of others and to entrust it to his closest friends.[41] But Cyrus' *philanthrôpia* is wedded to the goal of winning honor, whereas it is difficult to say whether Socrates is ever very concerned with winning honor for himself. In the *Memorabilia*, Socrates defends his decision to remain aloof from political office on the grounds that he can do a greater service to the city by training many young men for the role (1.6.15).

Finally, we may contrast Cyrus with a helping character from within the *Cyropaedia*, the Persian commoner Pheraulas, who debuts in Book Two when Cyrus proposes that all members of the army be rewarded according to their accomplishments in battle rather than by a uniform dispensation (2.3.7–16). After following Cyrus on campaign, Pheraulas becomes a wealthy and esteemed man. He is intelligent, loving of beauty and order, and careful to please Cyrus (8.3.5). He is so devoted (or deranged) that when a Sacian knight pelts him with a clod of dirt, he continues to deliver a message with a bloodied face, never pausing

[39] *Memorabilia* 1.2.60–61. This is the first extant coupling of *dêmotikos* with *philanthrôpos*. The adjective *dêmotikos* entails acting in a way agreeable or sympathetic to the people's wishes and interests, such as being friendly, obeying the laws (contrary to the tyrant's impulse), and being "non-oligarchic." Plutarch calls the Spartan king Agesilaus both *philanthrôpos* and *dêmotikos* for participating in the Spartan educational system (*agôgê*) rather than being raised as a privileged king (*Life of Agesilaus* 1.3.6). Evagoras is *dêmotikos* for his attentive care (*therapeia*) to the masses (Isocrates *Evagoras* 46). Xenophon's Cyrus, though not described as *dêmotikos*, may be seen as such for his attentive care to others, his upbringing in the Persian *agôgê*, his general ability to "blend in" with his fellow-citizens, and his dismissal of royal privileges (1.4.14). Cf. a similar portrayal of Cyrus the Younger's education (*Anabasis* 1.9.2). Herodotus' Cyrus, raised by a common woman, also fits this profile (*Histories* 113), as does the Argonaut Jason (Apollonius *Argonautica* 1.7). On Socrates' *philanthrôpia* cf. Plato *Euthyphro* 3d7.

[40] Elsewhere Xenophon calls Socrates "useful" (*ôphelimos*) to his friends: *Memorabilia* 3.7.1.3, 3.10.1.3, 4.1.1.5, 4.8.11.4.

[41] This practice begins in Cyrus' youth when he refuses to take back the gifts he had given to the Medes on their departure (1.4.26). He also refuses additional wealth from the Armenian king and he refuses the fortress of Gobryas and the gifts of Gadatas (3.1.42, 5.2.7–11, 5.4.29–32).

to address the injury.[42] That Pheraulas desires to benefit others is indicated by the faithful and abiding friendship he forms with the Sacian soldier (8.3.49–50). Nevertheless Pheraulas is not called a *philanthrôpos*. Xenophon describes him as having a *philetairetic* nature, something we might translate as "a sense of loyalty or devotion."[43] *philetaireia* seems to have an element of good will toward others, but less forethought and material benefaction than *philanthrôpia*. Xenophon says that Pheraulas, for his part, wanted nothing to do with the responsibility of vast wealth (8.3.40) and "loved the Sacian soldier because he was willing to manage everything" (8.3.50.6–7). Pheraulas is another example of someone who cares about helping others for the sake of friendship, in an apolitical context.

In sum, whatever we say about Cyrus' desire to help others, it does not seem to go so far as to help them selflessly, anonymously, indiscriminately, without honor, or without an opportunity to secure greater authority or responsibility for himself. His *philanthrôpia* is something grand and highly political. That said, we can still look for ways in which Cyrus' motives can be over-determined, that is, he might want both to win honor and to enjoy helping people *as an end in itself*. The first passage that gives direct insight into this question is a dinner scene in Book Seven where *philanthrôpia* is the topic of conversation. Banquets in the *Cyropaedia* often function as classrooms, with Cyrus sometimes playing the role of the student, gathering perspectives and intelligence from his inner circle of followers, and other times taking the role of the teacher. Sometimes his trusty comrade Chrysantas plays the "substitute teacher" for Cyrus, giving the impression that the course of action under discussion is more a product of group-thinking than Cyrus' own personal initiative. At one point Cyrus praises Chrysantas not only for his obedience but for his ability to look out for Cyrus' interests above and beyond specific orders. Much of this discussion happens by design. Xenophon says that Cyrus likes to keep these occasions charming but also conducive to some good.[44]

Thus, Cyrus converses about *philanthrôpia* with the Assyrian nobleman Gobryas after the two have worked together to capture Babylon.[45] Gobryas remarks that Cyrus seems to enjoy practicing *philanthrôpia* more than generalship (*strateia*). Cyrus explains that in practicing generalship he must do harm

---

[42] *Cyropaedia* 8.3.28. Cf. Gera 1993:173–183 on this scene.

[43] Cf. ὁ τρόπος φιλέταιρός, 8.3.49.1. This word occurs once elsewhere in Xenophon, in his encomium to the Agesilaus. Agesilaus would not make peace with Corinth or Thebes until they had restored their Spartan sympathizers. Agesilaus also attacked the Phleisians to restore their Spartan sympathizers. Both acts were done out of *philetaireia* (*Agesilaus* 2.21.7).

[44] *Cyropaedia* 2.2.1. On the symposium as a type-scene in the *Cyropaedia*, see Gera 1993:132–191, who notes a "pronounced didactic tendency in all the symposia" (133).

[45] For the historical Ugbaru, who seems to be the basis for Xenophon's Gobryas, see Briant 1996:41–42.

but in practicing *philanthrôpia* he only helps others.[46] This example in itself does not *prove* that Cyrus likes to help others for its own sake, but that given two paths to winning honor, warfare and munificence, he prefers the latter.

Others notice Cyrus' pleasure (*hêdonê*) in helping others. The Persian Pheraulas supports putting Cyrus in charge of distributing the spoils of war because Cyrus, he says, takes "more pleasure" in giving than he does in keeping something for himself (cf. ἥδιον, 2.3.12.6). The king of the Hyrcanians later makes a similar observation (cf. ἥδεσθαι, 5.1.28.8). In the midst of dividing the spoils of Lydia, a soldier speculates that Cyrus' generosity implies that he must be keeping a lot for himself, but another insists that Cyrus takes more pleasure in giving than acquiring.[47] As we have already noted, Cyrus also feels pity on several occasions, which suggests that Xenophon means to represent a direct interest in the well-being of others that, while often alloyed with Cyrus' own interests and ambitions, is still distinct from them.

As a young man, Cyrus is naturally affectionate.[48] He excels in satisfying the needs of his uncle, Cyaxares, and his grandfather, Astyages, because he takes exceeding "delight" in gratifying them.[49] While Cyrus is otherwise restrained in drinking, he is "thirsty" to gratify a Mede who would take a music-girl as his spoil (cf. διψῶ, 5.1.1.13). There is an Isocratean flavor to his *philanthrôpia*, which we see when the Athenian philosopher instructs the Cyprian king Nicocles on the proper disposition for helping others:

> One must be a lover of humanity (*philanthrôpos*) and a lover of the city: for it is impossible to govern horses or dogs or men or anything else well, unless a man *delight* in that which he has to direct his attention.[50]

To Nicocles 15

Yet we might believe that Cyrus' pleasure in helping others derives more from the *anticipation* of some honor or security for himself than from an immediate delight in causing another person to prosper (believing that happy followers will praise and protect their leaders). For example, Cyaxares admits in a

---

[46] Cyrus the Younger prefers the "philanthropic" art of farming to warfare (*Oeconomicus* 4.4–4.25).

[47] *Cyropaedia* 8.4.7. Cf. διδοὺς ... ἥδεται, 8.4.31.6. Cf. *Odyssey* 10.38–45 on the suspicion that a leader's greater spoils may arouse. Chrysantas also esteems Cyrus' good will (8.1.5), and Cyrus esteems Chrysantas' habit of delighting in helping him (ἐπί τε τοῖς ἐμοῖς καλοῖς πολὺ μᾶλλον ἐμοῦ ἀγάλλεται καὶ ἥδεται, 8.4.11.15–16). For the pleasure of giving over receiving as an expression of erotic love, cf. Xenophon *Symposium* 4.14.

[48] Cf. φύσει φιλόστοργος, 1.3.2.3; 1.4.3.11, 1.4.26–28. The only other "affectionate" figure so described in Xenophon is Agesilaus (cf. τὸ δὲ φιλόστοργον καὶ θεραπευτικὸν τῶν φίλων, 8.1.5).

[49] Cf. ὑπερέχαιρεν, 1.3.12.5. Cf. Cyrus the Younger's exceeding desire to please his friends (*Anabasis* 1.9.24).

[50] Cf. the similar sentiment in *Memorabilia* 2.6.35.

moment of envy that he would take greater *pleasure* in giving gifts to Cyrus than in receiving them from him because in failing to give he has lost face in front of his comrades (5.5.27.1). Thus the pleasure of giving need not be intrinsic; it may be felt by someone whose more basic pleasure lies in feeling superior.

We might also think that Cyrus merely *displays* pleasure in helping others in order to charm his followers.[51] Xenophon and his contemporaries were well aware of how a leader might give off an air of friendliness simply to advance his own interests. In the *Memorabilia* the painter, Parrhasius, admits that it is possible to capture a subject's soul by an imitation of their facial expressions, both friendly (*philphronôs*) and hateful (3.10.4). In a climactic scene in the *Anabasis,* the treacherous Persian satrap, Tissaphernes, wins over the Spartan general Clearchus by showing a friendly disposition (*philophronoumenos*).[52] Despite the misgivings of others in the Greek army, Tissaphernes lures Clearchus into a meeting and has him killed along with many others (*Anabasis* 2.5.27–34). According to Demosthenes, Philip of Macedon once drank with Theban ambassadors at a sacrificial banquet, treating them "philanthropically" with money and gifts, so that he might convince them to betray their fellow citizens (cf. φιλανθρωπευόμενος, *On the False Embassy* 139.6; cf. 140.4). In the same speech, Demosthenes criticizes Aeschines for seeking a self-interested peace with Philip under the pretense of the name of *philanthrôpia* (99.1). Aeschines himself says that feelings of *philanthrôpia* are easily aroused by the actor's art (*On the False Embassy* 15.8–9). In an especially indignant tone, Isocrates rails against the masses for their vulnerability to flattery and displays of good will and kindness. He thus cynically advises Timotheus:

> You see the nature of the masses, how they are disposed to various pleasures and therefore feel greater fondness for those who try to gratify them than those who benefit them, and for those who trick them with a smile and gestures of *philanthrôpia* more than those who serve them with cautiousness and dignity ... If you please them, they will judge whatever you do not by a standard of truth, but give you the benefit of the doubt, and they will overlook your mistakes and elevate what you do right to the stars. For that's how good will affects everyone.

> *Antidosis* 133–134

[51] Gray 2011:100–105 has a helpful discussion of seeming versus being in the *Cyropaedia*. She challenges the assumption that Xenophon means to be ironic when he said that Cyrus "seemed to be" a certain way.

[52] Cf. Aristotle *On Virtues and Vices* 1251b1–3. A host of gestures may express *philophrosunê*: a handshake, the tone of voice, a smile, a toast, sharing food, or giving a thoughtful gift (cf. Xenophon *Symposium* 1.10.5, Sophocles *Ajax* 751, Xenophon *Anabasis* 4.5.29.2, Xenophon *Symposium* 2.24.4, Xenophon *Anabasis* 4.5.32.1).

It is thus *conceivable* that Xenophon meant to fashion his Cyrus with similar gestures, making him into someone who succeeds at winning over others by *pretending* sympathy and rehearsing all the smiles, handshakes, toasts, and benefactions that can charm others without any sincere good will on the part of the performer. It is unlikely, however, given our direct window into Cyrus' emotional states, that Xenophon means to portray him with such pretenses.

It is even less likely that Xenophon would have felt the need to be subtle or delicate about describing Cyrus' supposed pretenses, given that they were such familiar ways to interpret fourth-century leaders.[53] Moreover, on his deathbed, Xenophon's Cyrus counts it as a prime component of his own happy life that he has witnessed his friends made happy by his own efforts (8.7.7.1). Most importantly for our investigation is the fact that he imagines pleasure in being reunited with the earth after death, since they are both *philanthrôpoi*:

> As to my body, my sons, whenever I am dead, neither place it on gold nor on silver nor anything else, but return it to the earth as soon as possible. For what is more blessed than this, to be mingled with the earth, which brings forth and nourishes all beautiful things and all good things? And, as I have otherwise been a *philanthrôpos*, now gladly (*hêdeôs*) would I be united with the benefactor of humankind.
>
> *Cyropaedia* 8.7.25

These dying confessions seem to be the best proof that Cyrus enjoys helping others as an end in itself,[54] and strongly suggest that the good will others *perceive* in Cyrus is in fact meant by Xenophon to be sincere.

Part of the genius of Cyrus' leadership, we could say, is that he so prudently combines his fondness for helping others with his own desire to be honored and accepted.[55] This is not to say that, from our perspective or even an ancient Greek perspective, Xenophon's Cyrus always achieves this coalescence (a question we will pursue in further chapters).

One particular instance bears brief mention here: Cyrus' employment of the eunuch Gadatas as a table-companion and close confidant. This arrangement is beneficial for Cyrus because, as he explains, eunuchs can still be courageous but are also exceedingly loyal since they do not have familial or romantic interests to divide them (7.5.59-65). This one instance is not *per se* a failure of Cyrus to

[53] Cf. Gray 2011:64–67.
[54] We should be clear: to say that Cyrus takes direct pleasure in helping others is not the same as saying that Cyrus takes pleasure *that others be helped by anyone*. This may not have been a distinction Xenophon thought to make.
[55] Cf. Danzig 2009:274–275, and forthcoming.

coalesce his interests with those of his followers since Cyrus had both rescued and avenged Gadatas, who felt intense gratitude. Xenophon explains that Cyrus made a regular practice of employing eunuchs, however, and it is not clear whether he chose men who had already been made into eunuchs elsewhere or caused them to be castrated. This problem is further complicated by the fact that, as offensive as it is to our own contemporary sensibility, it was possible to see the process of becoming a eunuch as "voluntary" and thus consistent with Cyrus' "philanthropic" practice of leading by "willing obedience."[56]

Cyrus' "philanthropic" death in Xenophon is much different from the one Herodotus gives him on the eastern extremes of the Persian Empire, battling queen Tomyris of the Massegetae, his head soaked in blood.[57] In fact, in both Herodotus and Ctesias, Cyrus' benefactions, such as they are, are limited to the Persian people (he is their liberator and as such their benefactor), whereas it is clear that Xenophon's Cyrus is beneficial to many nations. The *barbaroi* (not the Persians specifically) hail him as "*philanthrôpotatos,*" and he is the "father" to many nations.[58] Sancisi-Weerdenburg has observed that Cyrus' deathbed speech has many elements common to the speech of Darius' tomb inscriptions at Naqš-i Rustam, so much so as to suggest that Xenophon had become familiar with them through oral tradition. The elements include divine help in the king's success as well as his physical prowess, justice, and self-restraint.[59] Ctesias, too, preserves a much less-detailed final speech for his Cyrus (F9.8). But one of the elements missing from both of these accounts is this mention of the king as a benevolent benefactor; missing, too, is the specific association of Cyrus' *philanthrôpia* with the *philanthrôpia* of the earth. This association seems to be largely Xenophontic, or at least preserved by Xenophon independent of known sources. In the *Oeconomicus*, Ischomachus explains that farming is a "philanthropic" craft, dear to gods and men who are willing to study it.[60] Cyrus the Younger is praised for practicing the art of farming and for taking pride in it even more than in war.[61]

---

[56] See Bullough 2002:1–17, Llewellyn-Jones 2002:19–49, Azoulay 2004c.

[57] Gera 1993:244 points out as well that Xenophon's attention to Cyrus' burial is only one of two in the *Cyropaedia* (the other is the burial of Pantheia and Abradatas). There is no mention of Astyages', Cambyses', or Mandane's burial, whereas it is a regular feature of Ctesias' *Persica* to describe burials and monuments.

[58] *Cyropaedia* 1.2.1, 8.8.1. Cyrus is also called "father" in Herodotus, but only by the Persians (*Histories* 3.89).

[59] Sancisi-Weerdenburg 1985:448–453. Sancisi-Weerenburg's entire article is a good illustration of the challenges we face (as well as the possibilities) in speculating about the uses of Persian history and folklore in the *Cyropaedia*.

[60] *Oeconomicus* 15.4.2, 19.17.3. For this theme in Roman literature see Powell 1988:208–209.

[61] *Oeconomicus* 4.4–4.25. As we discussed above Cyrus the Elder enjoys practicing the art of *philanthrôpia* more than war (*Cyropaedia* 8.4.6–8). On the broader similarity between the two see Due 1989:187–192.

In the *Cyropaedia*, the Persian Pheraulas praises the earth's generosity and then amplifies that of Cyrus himself by comparison (8.3.38).

Philanthrôpia and Divinity

There is a further tendency elsewhere in Greek literature to associate *philanthrôpia* with divinity and then with leaders who are in a position to benefit others in grand ways. In the first extant use of superlative *philanthrôpia* (421 BCE), a Chorus in Aristophanes asks Hermes to help rescue the goddess Peace, praying to him as most generous and most "philanthropic."[62] As we noted above, it is also Aristophanes who in Plato's *Symposium* describes Eros as the "most philanthropic" of gods for being a physician to the ills brought on by erotic love (189d1). Not only does *philanthrôpia* in superlative form have divine connotations, but the earliest extant use of the *philanthrôp-* stem describes the god Prometheus when he gives fire to mortals (c. 430 BCE).[63] Whereas gods typically deal with mortals contractually,[64] Prometheus does so because of his "philanthropic" tendency (cf. φιλανθρώπου ... τρόπου, *Prometheus Bound* 11). The idea behind this tendency is captured earlier by Pindar (c. 470 BCE), who describes the divine centaur Cheiron as a wild creature "with a mind that is loving of men."[65] Isocrates explains how a mortal leader's *philanthrôpia* may be analogous to the divine when he encourages Philip of Macedon to emulate his ancestor Heracles' *philanthrôpia* toward the Greeks (*To Philip* 114.4).[66] He gives Philip further invitation to this divine pretension by explaining that good deeds, gentleness, and *philanthrôpia* win glory and reverence:

> Gods who are the source of good things for us are hailed as "Olympian," but those who are appointed for punishments and misfortunes receive rather unfriendly epithets. Private citizens and cities build temples and altars for the former, but the latter are honored neither in prayers nor in sacrifices, but we perform rites to banish them. You should condition

---

[62] Cf. ὦ φιλανθρωπότατε, *Peace* 393.

[63] Cf. Lorenz 1914:8-9, De Ruiter 1932:272, and Ferguson 1958:102-103. Cf. Nikolaidis 1980:351 on *philanthrôpia* and divinity.

[64] Cf. Chryses' prayer to Apollo in *Iliad* 1.37–43.

[65] Cf. νόον ἔχοντ' ἀνδρῶν φίλον, *Pythian Odes* 3.5. See Gera 1993:50. Cf. Prometheus' own "excessive love for mortals" (διὰ τὴν λίαν φιλότητα βροτῶν, *Prometheus Bound* 123). By contrast, *philandria* is often an erotic love for men (cf. Euripides *Andromache* 229), though contrast Thebes "man-loving plain" in a patriotic sense (cf. πέδον φίλανδρον, Aeschylus *Seven Against Thebes* 902).

[66] On Xenophon and Isocrates as pioneers in transitioning *philanthrôpia* from the divine to the mortal (leadership) realm, see Azoulay 2004b:319.

yourself with these things in mind and try to get everyone to have an even better opinion about you than they already do.

To Philip 117.1–118.3

Isocrates flatters the fourteen-year-old Alexander in a similar way when he praises him as "philanthropic" and a lover of Athens (*To Alexander* 2.1). Cyrus seems to be assuming the analogy between divine and leaderly *philanthrôpia* when he surrounds himself with pious friends (*theosebeis*), thinking that they would be less likely to commit crimes against one another or against him, "for he considered himself their benefactor" (8.1.25.8; cf. 3.3.4.3). The reasoning seems to be that just as Cyrus sees himself as a benefactor like the gods, he seeks to surround himself with those who knew how to revere such munificence.

In sum, divinities with *philanthrôpia* tend to help mortals in grand, civilizing, and permanent ways. Prometheus gives fire. Hermes helps rescue Peace from beneath a giant mound of stones. Cheiron teaches Asclepius the art of medicine, and the physician Eros cures mortals of lovesickness. Cronus is a "philanthropic" god for assigning nobler spirits to govern humanity (Plato *Laws* 713d6). For Xenophon's Socrates the gods provide humanity with everything from the sun and the earth to food and the capacity for reason—out of *philanthrôpia*.[67] Thus, in crafting a "philanthropic" theme to Cyrus' deathbed speech, Xenophon seems to be drawing upon his own associations of both farming and grand leadership. He also reflects the Greek tradition of seeing powerful leaders as able to help others in ways that approximate divine "philanthropic" grandeur. Such grand benefaction is captured in the encouragement that Cambyses gives the young Cyrus at the end of Book One as he sets off on a pursuit of the Assyrians that will net him an empire:

> To know how to organize other people so that they might have all the necessities in abundance and so that they might all be the kind of people they need to be, this certainly seemed to us worthy of admiration.[68]

Cyropaedia 1.6.7–9

Cyrus' *philanthrôpia* and *philotîmia* converge at the point of grandeur.

We conclude that while it is correct to see Cyrus' as highly motivated to win honor when he engages in helping others, it is incorrect to assume that loving honor (or some other manifestation of personal advantage) must necessarily taint, or even undermine, Cyrus' desire to help others—or that loving honor

---

[67] Xenophon *Memorabilia* 4.3.5.6, 4.3.7.7. Cf. Martin 1961:174, Nikolaidis 1980:352n17 on *philanthrôpia* as a civilizing behavior.

[68] Cf. the similar sentiment from Socrates (*Memorabilia* 3.6.3).

is Cyrus' only motive or even his strongest motive. He is not like Achilles, for example, who seems to see his contributions to the Achaean army at Troy, at least at times, as primarily contractual: honor and glory in return for service in reclaiming Helen for Menelaus (*Iliad* 1.149–171, though cf. 9.323–327). By contrast, Xenophon presents *philanthrôpia* and *philotîmia* as distinct though concurrent expressions of Cyrus' soul (1.2.1). He affirms their distinctiveness when he says that Cyrus helped his age-mates secure favors for their fathers from Astyages, *both out of a love of being honored and a fondness for others*. This foregoing discussion of *philanthrôpia* challenges the view that Cyrus is primarily selfish or that he manipulates others for his own ends. One might still argue that Cyrus' love for others is somehow eclipsed by his love for honor, but it is difficult to dispute the claim that a love for others, in and of itself, is a large part of Cyrus' character and thus a large part of Xenophon's Theory of Leadership.

Conclusion

We have sought to identify a number of features to Cyrus' *philanthrôpia* and *philotîmia*, both of which are rich, multi-faceted concepts. *Philanthrôpia* is for Xenophon a fondness for humans that involves feelings of pity, sympathy, affection, and care. It entails gift-giving, tokens of honor, matchmaking, and attention to illness. It may be grand, civilizing, and long-lasting, coming as it does with associations of divinity. *Philotîmia* is a love of being honored, but more than just a desire for tokens of distinction. It is often a love of being praised, approved of, or appreciated. Cyrus wants others to feel the fondness for him that he feels for others. Additionally, the love of being honored is a love for the highest honors (*megalopsychia*) in every important agonistic theater.

We have seen further that in his *philanthrôpia* and *philotîmia* Cyrus plays at being a king from a very young age. He imagines himself as the "ruler" of Sacas, the Medan king's closest companion, granting or denying access to all who would see him. He disperses prizes at the dinner table to worthy servants and may be seen as the "founder" of this practice among the Persians. He gives a cloak to one of his contemporaries to mark him out as his favorite, just as his grandfather had honored Cyrus himself. He takes greater risks than those around him think appropriate. He aims for the highest honors, like hunting all the animals of the world, regardless of censure and punishment. Contrary to the accounts of the young Cyrus in Herodotus and Ctesias, these flirtations with kingship do not involve taking advantage of others, conquering, or humiliating them. Instead, others win honor and distinction along with Cyrus and are encouraged to do as he does. In the following Chapter we will explore the ways in which Cyrus' love of learning (*philomatheia*) fits into this picture.

2

Curiosity, Aptitude, and Intense Awareness

A S WE HAVE SEEN, Cyrus' *philanthrôpia* and *philotîmia* are intimately
connected. How does Cyrus' *philomatheia* (love of learning) fit in? Our investigation will entail a survey of Xenophon's treatments of learning elsewhere,
especially in the *Oeconomicus*, *Memorabilia*, and *Anabasis*, but we will begin with
the *Cyropaedia*. Aside from Xenophon's summary statement on Cyrus' three
superlative traits, *philomatheia* first appears in 1.4. There, Xenophon describes
the many reasons for Cyrus' chattiness (*polylogia*):

> Καὶ ἦν μὲν ἴσως πολυλογώτερος, ἅμα μὲν διὰ τὴν παιδείαν, ὅτι
> ἠναγκάζετο ὑπὸ τοῦ διδασκάλου καὶ διδόναι λόγον ὧν ἐποίει καὶ
> λαμβάνειν παρ' ἄλλων, ὁπότε δικάζοι, ἔτι δὲ καὶ διὰ τὸ φιλομαθὴς εἶναι
> πολλὰ μὲν αὐτὸς ἀεὶ τοὺς παρόντας ἀνηρώτα πῶς ἔχοντα τυγχάνοι, καὶ
> ὅσα αὐτὸς ὑπ' ἄλλων ἐρωτῷτο, διὰ τὸ ἀγχίνους εἶναι ταχὺ ἀπεκρίνετο,
> ὥστ' ἐκ πάντων τούτων ἡ πολυλογία συνελέγετο αὐτῷ.

> He was perhaps a little too chatty because of his youth, in that he was
> compelled by his teacher both to give an explanation of what he was
> doing and to receive one from others whenever he judged a case; more-
> over, he himself was always asking for explanations of things because
> he was *philomathês*, and as often as he himself was questioned by others,
> he would quickly answer because of his keen wit, such that a chatty
> disposition took hold of him from all these sources.

Cyropaedia 1.4.3.1–9

The first thing to note about Cyrus' *philomatheia* is that it seems to be a natural
curiosity. I say, "natural," because Xenophon does not attribute Cyrus' inquisitiveness to any encouragement he receives from others, nor does it seem to
be influenced by particular interests. The young Cyrus is merely interested in
having the causes of things explained to him. To this extent he is like Plato's
Philosopher King, who is both a *philomathês* and a lover of wisdom (*philosophos*).

This is the only instance, however, where Cyrus' curiosity is portrayed as open-ended, without any ulterior motive or particular field.

Instead, when he visits Astyages in Media, Cyrus is outfitted with fancy clothes and given a horse, which he takes exceeding pleasure in learning to ride (cf. μανθάνων ὑπερέχαιρεν, 1.3.3.6).[1] Xenophon explains that this delight derives from Cyrus' love of beauty and love of being honored. Later, his love of learning horsemanship manifests itself in Cyrus' competitiveness with his Medan age-mates and his decision to remain in Media despite his mother's protestations (1.3.15). Cyrus is curious to learn to hunt and eagerly asks his elders what animals he should and should not pursue (cf. 1.4.7.6, 1.4.8.1). That Cyrus loves to learn about the hunt *for its own sake* is implied by the killer instinct he shows at the moment he spots his first wild deer and then a boar, which he pursues regardless of all that he had been taught, despite the danger (1.4.8). Clearly, he also hopes to win honor and to benefit his friends because he shares the meat from the hunt (1.4.10).

When Cyrus learns from his father that the art of hunting may be applied to warfare, he studies this subject, too. Cambyses explains that *philomatheia* in war entails not only learning the traditional strategies against an enemy but also devising new ones (1.6.38.). Due has noted the thorough attention that Xenophon pays to military tactics and innovations in equipment and weaponry.[2] For his part, Cyrus devises a new style of chariot (6.1.28), introduces Persian commoners to the army (2.1.9), and even observes how his troops invent new tactics (2.3.17–20). Cyrus is obviously interested in warfare for the purpose of winning glory but, as in the hunt, he sometimes participates in battle for its own sake and even irrationally, like a "noble but inexperienced hunting-dog" (1.4.21–22).

There is precedence for curiosity in Persian kings in Herodotus, but a morbid one. Herodotus' Cyrus places the conquered Croesus on the pyre, either as an offering to the gods or because he "desired to know if some god would save him from being burned alive" (*Histories* 1.86). Cyrus' son, Cambyses, shows a similar morbid curiosity after his conquest of Egypt. Herodotus says that Cambyses "made trial of the king Psamminitus' soul" by marching his daughter as a slave in front of him and then marching his son off to be executed (3.14). When Psamminitus shows no reaction to these atrocities but instead bursts into tears at the sight of an old friend reduced to poverty, he becomes an object of wonder to Cambyses.

---

[1] Cyrus' comrade Chrysantas (who is in many ways a Cyrus-in-the-making) shares a pleasure in learning to ride (4.3.15).

[2] Due 1989:181–182. Cf. Briant 1996:19–20 on the likelihood that these innovations were made by Cyrus.

The only trial of character that Xenophon's Cyrus makes is of the conquered Armenian king. Yet, his investigation is not conducted out of morbid curiosity, but in accordance with his ethical curiosity and political ambition.[3] When Tigranes appeals to him to defend his father, Cyrus acquiesces, knowing that Tigranes had studied under a sophist who had won his admiration. Cyrus "strongly desires" to hear whatever he had to say and enthusiastically tells him to speak whatever he knows.[4] Tigranes proceeds to convince Cyrus that the Armenian king has learned self-restraint (something fear and respect can induce) and that he would be a valuable ally to the Medes. Thus, Cyrus accomplishes his primary goal–securing tribute and reinforcements from the Armenians–and even makes them into friends by virtue of his gentleness and wisdom (3.1.41). In his desire to hear profitable speeches, Cyrus follows the example of Isocrates more than Herodotus. Isocrates explains in a letter to the Cyprian Demonicus:

> If you are *philomathês*, then you will be a learner of many things. Maintain what you know with practice; but what you have not learned, grasp with understanding. For it is equally shameful to hear a useful account and not to learn it as it is to fail to take some good gift from friends. Spend your leisure time in life in *the love of hearing accounts of things*. For in this way discoveries difficult for others to make will turn out easy to learn for you.
>
> *To Demonicus* 18

In addition to his eagerness to hear Tigranes in the trial of the Armenian king, Cyrus asks for intelligence reports throughout his campaign. He also has the modesty to ask for counter-proposals to what he himself proposes.[5] In addition to a willingness to hear proposals from others (a practice that might seem designed only to build concord among the group), Cyrus seeks to know things from his followers and values their contributions. He praises Chrysantas not only for his obedience and good will, but also for the way Chrysantas advises him and modifies his orders according to whatever Chrysantas understands to be better (8.4.11). When Cyrus prepares to appear in his first public procession

---

[3] Cf. Cyrus the Younger's less philosophically-minded trial of Orontas (*Anabasis* 1.6.4–11).

[4] Cf. πάνυ ἐπεθύμει, 3.1.14.6. Tatum 1989:138 sees the Tigranes episode as part of Cyrus' staging of his mercy for the Armenians and his interest in Tigranes' speech as "mainly a literary curiosity." This is, I believe, an attempt to ascribe a level of manipulation and intentionality to Cyrus that Xenophon gives little indication of.

[5] *Cyropaedia* 4.5.24, 6.2.24, 6.2.39, 6.3.36, 6.4.19, 7.5.7, 7.5.37. Cf. Jason and Hypsipyle's gentleness in assemblies in the *Argonautica* (1.657–701, 3.171–175). Contrast their behavior with Agamemnon's ungentle disregard for the opinions of the Achaeans and Chryses (*Iliad* 1.22–32).

in Babylon, he explains how he imagines the procession should go, but also asks his comrades to "teach" him a better way if need be:

> If then it seems to any of you nobler to process in a way other than as we would now, explain it to me (διδασκέτω με) when we return. For everything must be arranged in the way that seems noblest and best to you.
>
> *Cyropaedia* 8.3.2.5–8

In the same spirit as Herodotus' Cyrus, who keeps the conquered Croesus and Astyages in close company, Xenophon's Cyrus not only spares Croesus but employs him as a counselor.[6]

Cyrus' intellectual interests strongly resemble those of his descendant, Cyrus the Younger. The younger Cyrus was "most kingly" (*basileukotatos*), Xenophon explains, because of his exceptional achievements in horsemanship, warfare, and hunting compared to his Persian age-mates:

> He seemed to be ... most loving of horses and best at managing them. They also deemed him most curious about the arts of war (*philomathes-tatos*), namely in using the bow and spear, and most diligent at practicing them. And when it befit his age, he was most loving of the hunt and in fact most loving of danger in regard to wild beasts.[7]
>
> *Anabasis* 1.9.5.2–6.3

This is the final of the four uses of the *philomath-* stem in Xenophon, and it again seems to have application to a specific field. Xenophon does not treat all forms of the "love of learning" as pleasurable in themselves, though certain subjects may be so. In this respect Xenophon disagrees with Plato's Socrates, who says that a lover of something must be a lover of *all aspects* of something, whether the person in question is a lover of a person or a lover of honor (*Republic* 474c–475e). As lovers of learning, both of Xenophon's Cyruses seem to love learning specific subjects more than the learning itself.

---

[6] *Cyropaedia* 7.2.29. Cyrus does the same with the Hyrcanian king (4.5.23–25). Cf. Briant 1996:33 for the political advantages of this practice in Near Eastern culture.

[7] Herodotus has a similar picture of the Persian educational system (*Histories* 1.136). Plutarch reports that the Magi also instructed young Persians (*Life of Artaxerxes* 3.3). Cf. Sancisi-Weerdenburg 1987:39.

The same is true of Xenophon's Socrates, who disdains cosmology and natural science in favor of ethics and leadership.[8] Accordingly, he sought pupils whose love of learning was directed at ethical, political, and domestic lessons:

> He would take as proof of their good natures the swiftness of learning (ἐκ τοῦ ταχύ τε μανθάνειν) whatever they paid attention to and the remembrance of what they learned and *the desire of all the lessons* (ἐπιθυμεῖν τῶν μαθημάτων πάντων) by which it is possible to operate a household and a city nobly and to manage well, in sum, human beings and human affairs.
>
> *Memorabilia* 4.1.2.4–8

Socrates himself regards pleasure in learning a subject (farming) as the basis of philosophy:

> First this, Ischomachus, I said, I think I would gladly learn (ἡδέως μανθάνειν)—*for that is especially the character of the lover of wisdom*—how I might work the land, should I wish, and harvest the most barley and wheat.
>
> *Oeconomicus* 16.9

From the foregoing examples, it would seem that Xenophon's understanding of the love of learning is not generally open-ended; only in limited ways does it seem to be learning for its own sake. We might say, for example, that Cyrus loves learning to hunt as an end in itself (since he pursues it so monomaniacally) but also as a means of winning honor, as evidenced by the fact that he is eager to share the spoils of the hunt with his grandfather and friends.

Aptitude for Learning

Rather than a strict *love* of learning, *philomatheia* seems to be a propensity or aptitude for learning, two manifestations of which are the ability to excel in contests of learning and to pick up lessons quickly. We recall Xenophon's descriptions of Cyrus the Younger's excellence in learning to ride a horse and of the quick-learning Socratic pupil. These features of learning are treated in accounts of Cyrus outside Xenophon, too. Whereas Ctesias does not describe any interaction between Cyrus and his Medan contemporaries, he does show

---

8 *Memorabila* 1.1.11–15. The contrast between Xenophon's and Plato's portrayal of Socrates vis-à-vis topics of interest was thought in the ancient world to be evidence of a tension between the two thinkers (Aulus Gellius *Attic Nights* 14.3.5).

the ways in which Cyrus, starting out from a family of goatherds,[9] worked his way into Astyages' court. Cyrus' progression seems to be a kind of hierarchical education for the low-born. The Ctesian Cyrus advances as a slave from external palace decorator to interior decorator to lamp-bearer until he become so distinguished that he lands the prestigious job of wine-pourer to the king's dining companions. The chief supervisor in this version is Artembares,[10] who serves as Cyrus' mentor and eventually his adoptive father. He observes how Cyrus pours wine attentively and gracefully and thus appoints him to be his successor. It is from this point that Cyrus comes to win favor from Astyages and eventually plots the liberation of Persia from Media.

Xenophon's Cyrus also plays at being a cup-bearer and seems to excel at it as much as Ctesias' Cyrus.[11] Just as he learns the character lessons of his Persian education "by observation," so does he mimic the wine-pourer Sacas "just as he as observed him" (cf. 1.2.8, 1.3.9). Just as Ctesias' Cyrus rises from the lowest ranks of the Persian goatherds by learning newer and more important roles, so does Xenophon's Cyrus become the best student in the company of the other Persian elites because he learns *quickly* all that is necessary (1.3.1).

In fact, much of what Xenophon's Cyrus does as a youth evinces a mental ease and quickness, guided by a high capacity for empathy. In our discussion in Chapter One on Cyrus' ability to blend in with his contemporaries, we saw how he "quickly" came to be on familiar terms with them and "quickly" won over their fathers (1.4.1). He also "quickly" declares his intent to remain in Media when his mother asks him to decide, which might at first seem to be indicative of impulsiveness until Cyrus thoughtfully explains that it is the best opportunity to learn to ride (1.3.15). Again, Cyrus answers "quickly" when his teachers question him, a contributing factor to his chattiness (1.4.3). In a triplet of quickness, Cyrus equals and surpasses his comrades at horsemanship; then on the hunt he exhausts the supply of animals in his grandfather's preserve (cf. ταχὺ ... ταχὺ ... ταχὺ, 1.4.5).

Cyrus' *philomatheia* involves not only a general desire to learn, but a desire to learn specific honorific subjects (horsemanship, hunting, warfare, ethics,

---

[9] Ctesias F8d*1–7. On Cyrus as a "king from humble beginnings," adapted from the Sargon myth, see Drews 1974.

[10] In Herodotus Artembares is the father of the upper-class Medan boy who was whipped by Cyrus (*Histories* 1.114–116). In Ctesias Artembares is Astyages' cupbearer and may have been his eunuch since there is a Near Eastern tradition of conflating the two roles. In Xenophon Sacas seems to play the double role of Astyages' wine-pourer and harem guard (*Cyropaedia* 1.3.11). Llewellyn-Jones 2002:24 suggests that the Greek *oinoxoos* and *eunouxos* may have been interchangeable.

[11] Gera 1993:156–157 plausibly suggests that Xenophon, with his version of Cyrus becoming "his own" Sacas may be "explaining" how Ctesias could come to tell of Cyrus as the actual cupbearer to Astyages.

politics). Additionally, it involves a certain aptitude or inclination to observe, process, and emulate those around him, which presupposes a high capacity for empathy if not sympathy, that is, a high emotional intelligence. This is not to say that Cyrus' observations are always correctly processed; for example, he assumes that the wine-pourer, Sacas, is poisoning Astyages and his friends because they become intoxicated from the wine he serves (1.3.10).

Xenophon seems to be drawing his formulation of Cyrus' *philomatheia* not only from fourth-century Greek conceptions of it (especially Socrates, as Xenophon understood him), but also from his understanding of the Persian education. By being "most loving of learning" (*philomathestatos*), Cyrus becomes "best in his class," just like his descendent Cyrus the Younger. Finally, since Xenophon claims that Cyrus was celebrated *in Persian lore* as *philomathestatos* (1.2.1), he may be drawing from a tradition (preserved in some form by Ctesias) of a legendary figure and man of the people, who worked his way into the highest political positions by his aptitude for learning (e.g. quickly imitating and mastering various roles along a *cursus honorum*). This tradition may explain why Xenophon says that Cyrus is "celebrated" in song as a most exceptional learner.

Paying Attention

One term for describing Cyrus' mental activity is so closely related to *philomatheia* as to be synonymous with it. As we noted above, Cyrus the Younger was *philomathestatos* at learning the arts of war. He was also "most attentive" in practicing them (*meletêrotatos*). Similarly, our Cyrus is described as being *philomathês* about the affairs of war; he is eager to know all about them. This behavior suggests a certain "awareness" or "attentiveness" to all the questions that need to be answered. The trait that typically describes someone with this awareness in Xenophon is *epimeleia*. As *philomatheia* is the disposition to investigate, we might think of *epimeleia* is the *exercise* of that disposition on particular subjects. It is to the curious mind what work is to the vigorous body: just as loving to be honored entails a love of labor (1.2.1), so the love of learning seems to entail "loving to pay attention." Socrates says in the *Memorabilia* that the general and estate manager both need to be attentive and lovers of toil in their affairs (cf. καὶ ἐπιμελεῖς καὶ φιλοπόνους 3.4.9.6).

Attentiveness is an apparently prosaic leadership trait, but Xenophon prizes it highly, and we would do well to note its pervasiveness in his Theory of Leadership. Not only is attentiveness to individual matters required, but a *comprehensive* awareness of all facets of an endeavor. For example, Cambyses advises Cyrus on the eve of his expedition against the Assyrians that the leader must pay attention to strategy as well as to the overall needs of the troops (resources, wealth, and military strength), much as an estate manager must oversee all facets of a household.[12] Cambyses says Cyrus must be especially attentive to the health of his followers (cf. ἡ τῆς ὑγιείας ἐπιμέλεια, 1.6.16.4). While on campaign Cyrus applies these recommendations first by interrogating his uncle, Cyaxares, about the nature of his army and then by looking for information from every available source (2.1.2–8). When Cyrus comes to rule Babylon, he allots leisure time to attend to the most important affairs of state (cf. ἐπιμελεῖσθαι, 8.1.13.3). He applies the metaphors of the household manager and military commander by paying attention to the revenues of the empire and organizing it according to the units of the army. This arrangement leaves him more free time than someone watching over a single house or ship (8.1.15).

As Cambyses explains, the leader's attentiveness requires losing sleep while taking thought for all the contingencies of a campaign:

> You must understand this very well, that all the men you should count on to obey you, will count on you to take thought on their behalf. So don't ever be senseless, but during the night plan out what your followers will do when the day arrives and during the day plan out how the affairs of the night will be best.

Cyropaedia 1.6.42

The tradition of the "wakeful leader" in Greek literature goes back to Homer's *Iliad*, where Cambyses' sentiment is first articulated by Dream, who stresses the importance of paying attention to the sleeping Agamemnon:

> You are asleep, son of war-like Atreus, tamer of horses! A counsel-giving man ought not sleep the whole night, someone to whom a host has been entrusted and for whom there are so many concerns. Now quickly pay attention to me![13]

Iliad 2.23–26

After stressing the importance of paying attention, Cambyses proceeds to explain to Cyrus, in laborious detail, what such a degree of attention would consist of. Like Isocrates to the studious Demonicus, he says that Cyrus must be a learner of many things:

---

12 *Cyropaedia* 1.6.9–12. Cf. Cyrus carrying out some of these instructions (6.1.23–24) and Socrates' similar litany of challenges facing the cavalry commander (*Memorabilia* 3.3).

13 Agamemnon's inattentive sleep is emphatic in this context because Zeus is portrayed as pondering and wakeful (2.1–4). Agamemnon redeems himself somewhat on the eve of the Doloneia when he is portrayed as wakeful while others are asleep (10.1–4).

How you must draw up the army for battle; or how to lead it during the day or night, or along narrow roads or wide, or hilly paths or plains; or how to make camp; or how to set up night watches or day watches; or how to attack the enemy or retreat from them; or how to lead past a hostile city; or how to attack a wall or retreat from it; or how to cross glens or rivers; or how to protect the cavalry, or the spearmen or the bowmen; and if in fact the enemy should suddenly appear before you as you are leading the flanks, you must plan out how you must make your stand; and if the enemy should appear from somewhere else other than head-on as you are leading the phalanx, you must plan out how you should turn against them; or how you might best discover the plans of the enemy; or how the enemy might least come to know yours.

Cyropaedia 1.6.42–43

Cambyses acknowledges that Cyrus already knows that these questions are important; the key is to ask them throughout the campaign:

But why should I tell you all these things? For whatever I myself know, you have often heard, and you have not been ignorant or neglected anyone who seemed to know any of these things. So I think you must apply these questions to the circumstances, however each of them seems advantageous to you.

Cyrus follows Cambyses' advice throughout his campaign. Xenophon portrays him as continually restless in monitoring his army: "he himself in fact did not occupy one place but he rode around, now here, now there, looking out and paying attention to see if the army needed anything."[14] Even in his youth, Cyrus shows this inquisitiveness and wakefulness. As soon as Cyrus learns of the encroachment that the Assyrians have made on Medan territory, he dons his armor and joins his grandfather, to his astonishment (1.4.18). Once Cyrus takes a survey of the situation, he poses a series of questions and then advocates making a charge upon the enemy, at first against Astyages' better judgment (note again Cyrus' "kingly" daring). He eventually prevails upon his grandfather who again marvels at Cyrus' "sensibility and wakefulness" (cf. καὶ ἐφρόνει καὶ ἐγρηγόρει, 1.4.20.2). Later among his Persian contemporaries the young Cyrus wins a reputation for outstanding diligence toward his lessons (1.5.1). The payoff of attentiveness is more than mental: on the eve of their first battle with the Assyrians, Cyrus inspires his men with the assurance that he has been "observing" their valor since childhood (1.5.7).

---

[14] Cf. ἐφεώρα τε καὶ ἐπεμελεῖτο, 5.3.59.3; cf. 6.1.24.

The role that paying attention plays in proper leadership, while implicit in these previous examples, is made explicit in several other places in the *Cyropaedia*. Cambyses declares that attentive people live more securely than those who are off their guard (cf. ἐπιμελουμένους, 1.6.5). Cyrus himself stresses the importance of attentiveness to his followers (1.5.11.10–11) and in particular for keeping their empire secure:

> Those [in possession of an empire] must not become careless (ἀμελεῖν) nor abandon themselves to instant pleasure. For I think it is a great achievement to have acquired an empire but a far greater one to preserve it once acquired. For the acquisition of empire often falls to the man who shows only daring, but keeping the empire that has been acquired no longer happens without self-control, self-mastery, and *much attentiveness* (πολλῆς ἐπιμελείας).
>
> *Cyropaedia* 7.5.76

By showing that he observes all of his followers' behavior, Cyrus instills an intense *philotîmia* in them. Because of their constant practice, they together perform every kind of noble deed (8.1.39). Because of his great memory, Cyrus learns the names of his followers and oversees the selection of his closest associates.[15] Xenophon says that Cyrus saw good leaders as "a law with eyes," not only able to give instruction like the written law but also able to observe transgressors and punish them.[16]

Epimeleia even enhances Cyrus' ability to practice *philanthrôpia*. Cyrus' attentiveness in providing food and water to his slaves wins him the title father (8.1.44). Not only does Cyrus far surpass others in the *value* of the gifts he gives (which Xenophon says is not surprising) but in the nurturing care and attentiveness he shows to his friends.[17] In general, whenever someone is sick, Cyrus visits and provides whatever is needed, a preparation he made even in youth on campaign (8.2.25, 1.6.15).

Xenophon features *epimeleia* in the *Oeconomicus*, giving it as prominent a role in the art of farming as he does in generalship and kingship. The estate manager, Ischomachus says, increases his estate by being attentive and not lax (11.12.6). Estate managers fail at producing grain, wine, and fruit because they "do not care" to go through the steps necessary to produce them (20.4.2, 4.4, 4.6). Successful generals, too, differ from unsuccessful ones not in intelligence but in *attentiveness* (20.6.4). For estate managers and for leaders in general, oversight is

---

[15] Cf. μνημονικῶς 5.3.46–47, ὀνομαστὶ 1.4.15.5, 8.1.10.3.

[16] *Cyropaedia* 8.1.22. Cf. Cyrus the Younger's attention to justice (*Anabasis* 1.9.13).

[17] Cf. τῇ θεραπείᾳ καὶ τῇ ἐπιμελείᾳ τῶν φίλων, 8.2.13.2. Cf. Cyrus the Younger (*Anabasis* 1.9.24).

crucial to instilling a love of labor and a love of honor in the followers (12.19.4). Ischomachus quotes the Persian king that "the master's eye" is key to the accomplishment of any noble works (12.20.6, cf. 21.5). Cyrus the Younger, he says, pays attention to farming and warfare as the noblest of pursuits.[18] He, too, travels around his country and oversees as much of it as possible and what he cannot see himself he learns about through reports (4.8). The consistent refrain of the *Oeconomicus* is that the knowledge required to lead depends more on attentiveness than intelligence or ingenuity. Ischomachus insists that the art of farming is "most easy to learn" (15.4.5). Socrates, too, says that both geometry and astronomy are easy to acquire, insofar as they are of practical importance for travel, telling time, or setting night-watches.[19] Attentiveness can even add to someone's natural allotment of courage.[20] For Cyrus' father, Cambyses, attentiveness is the foundation of wisdom (recall that pleasure in learning is the foundation of philosophy for Socrates). When he tells Cyrus that the best path to seeming to be wise is actually being wise, he explains, "it is more characteristic of the wiser man to be attentive to what is needed than to be neglectful" (1.6.23).

One final aspect of awareness that we should note is Cyrus' awareness of *himself*. There are at least three instances where we can see this introspection at work. In Book Five, Cyrus has a lengthy dialogue on the power of love (*erôs*) with Araspas, who has been put in charge of the Susan noblewoman, Pantheia. Araspas urges Cyrus to behold her beauty, arguing that since love is a matter of free will, Cyrus will be immune to it. Cyrus declines, arguing on the contrary that he knows that *erôs* has the power to make him vulnerable to Pantheia's beauty (5.1.8). Unconvinced, Araspas ignores the risk and attends Pantheia until he is smitten with her common kindness to him. *Erôs* leads Araspas to force himself on Pantheia and almost costs him his life, but for Cyrus' gentleness and understanding. His folly serves as a pointed contrast to Cyrus' prudent self-awareness.

Beyond the dangers of love, Cyrus worries about his propensity for greed. He admits to Croesus, "I myself cannot overcome this thing which the gods have put into the souls of humans and which renders us all impoverished in the same way, but I too am insatiate of wealth just like others" (8.2.20). He explains that the only way he overcomes his greed is by not hoarding his wealth but rather giving it to his friends, thereby winning safety (*asphaleia*) and a good reputation

---

[18] *Oeconomicus* 4.4.6. Xenophon gives some indication that Persian youths were taught farming or at least "the powers of the products of the earth that were useful and harmful" (8.8.14).

[19] Cf. τοῦτο ῥᾴδιον εἶναι μαθεῖν, *Memorabilia* 4.7.2.6; ταῦτα δὲ ῥᾴδια εἶναι μαθεῖν, 4.7.4.7. Socrates shows a general confidence that, though ignorant, a motivated person may seek out others with the knowledge that is required (3.4.4).

[20] *Memorabilia* 3.9.1–2. Isocrates' Evagoras shares many features of attentiveness in Xenophon (*Evagoras* 41–44).

(*eukleia*). Cyrus contrasts with Croesus, who had made war on him despite being warned by the Delphic oracle to "know thyself," (i.e. to know his limitations as a general) (7.2.20). After his defeat, Croesus admits that he had been spoiled by wealth, bribes, and the flattery of those who claimed he would become the greatest of men by making war on Cyrus. Ultimately Croesus realizes that he did not know himself (7.2.23).

This presentation of self-knowledge is, we might say, both Socratean and *anti*-Herodotean. In the *Memorabilia* Socrates emphasizes the importance and means of acquiring self-knowledge (and of avoiding self-delusion), also citing the Delphic Oracle (4.2.24–30, 3.7.9). Herodotus' Cyrus is initially aware of his own mortality when he sees Croesus, a proud king like himself, about to be burnt on the pyre. Nevertheless his success eventually leads him to think of himself as "something more than human" and invincible in war (*Histories* 1.86, 1.204). This delusion of grandeur directly contributes to his downfall: he attempts to extend the Persian Empire to the Massagetae and is soundly defeated, his head soaked in blood.

Unlike his counterpart in Herodotus, Xenophon's Cyrus is continually wary that he could become fearful, proud, or recklessly happy. In one exhortation to his men on the eve of the great battle with the Assyrians, he hedges against living a completely virtuous life by vowing never "willingly" to do anything wicked or shameful (cf. ἑκών, 7.1.13.6). Cyrus later explains on his deathbed that one reason for his success was "my abiding fear that at some point in time I might see or hear or suffer something problematic. This fear prevented me from thinking excessively proud thoughts or feeling extravagant delight" (8.7.7). It is as if Xenophon's Cyrus "remembers" what happened to himself in Herodotus. And for all the connotations of divinity in his *philanthrôpia* (Chapter One, pp. 42–44), Cyrus is aware of his mortal vulnerability, which may be linked to his high capacity for pity.[21]

The extreme importance in Xenophon for any type of leader to pay attention—to himself, to his followers, to the enemy, to the land—seems to explain the emphasis he places on Cyrus' *philomatheia*. This trait suggests curiosity, inquisitiveness, and an aptitude for learning, especially about moral and political subjects, beyond any special keenness or genius (though Cyrus shows signs of these at times as well). In short, Cyrus does not display the epic cleverness of Odysseus or Oedipus' ability to solve riddles or the Philosopher King's conceptual brilliance, but these mental skills do not seem to matter as much

---

[21] See Sandridge 2007.

to Xenophon's vision of the best leadership.[22] At any rate, they are not funda-mental but may be the product of curiosity and attentiveness.

Conclusion

Here we conclude what we have thus far discovered about Cyrus' three superla-tive traits of character. *Philanthrôpia*, loosely translated as a "love of humanity," is more precisely a fondness for others, for mingling with them, taking pleasure in their company, and being concerned with their well-being. It may involve showing signs of encouragement or sympathy in good fortune or bad, gestures of attentive care to the sick or wounded, gentleness, affection, match-making, and gift-giving and benefaction, often on a grand and civilizing scale, such that it may be appropriate to call it "divine." Cyrus' *philotîmia* is in part a love of being honored by the community at large, but Xenophon often portrays it as a desire for popularity or approval from those in Cyrus' close company, e.g. his father, his grandfather, his uncle, his Medan and Persian contemporaries. This desire for popularity, however, may involve acts of daring and risk-taking (especially in hunting, warfare, and personal expenditure) beyond what others deem safe and thus marks Cyrus as a character of lofty ambition (*megalopsychia*) and worthy of royal sovereignty. Cyrus' *philomatheia* is a desire and aptitude to master subjects that bring honor, and seems to entail an abiding attentiveness (*epimeleia*), espe-cially in the form of self-awareness.

As we noted in the introduction, there are five different contexts within which we may understand Cyrus' character traits, namely, the Greek literary tradition, Greek historiographers of Persia, Xenophon's other writings, the writings of other fourth-century Athenians, and Persian history, insofar as we can recover it from inscriptions and artifacts or infer it from an oral tradition embedded in Xenophon but different from what Herodotus and Ctesias report. It is one thing to say that these contexts exist and to believe that they all play a critical role in Xenophon's depiction of Cyrus. It is much more difficult, however, to say exactly how and to what extent they do play this role, and we have tried to proceed with due caution in explaining the various sources for Xenophon's characterization of Cyrus.

Having examined the form and meaning of Cyrus' three superlative traits of soul, we will now assess their *fundamentality* to other traits in Xenophon's Theory of Leadership.

---

[22] To the extent that Cyrus' great leadership lies in his ability to establish new institutions he resembles the wise Lycurgus in the *Constitution of the Lacedaemonians* (1.2).

3

On the Fundamentality of *Philanthrôpia, Philomatheia,* and *Philotîmia*

To DETERMINE THE FUNDAMENTALITY of Cyrus' superlative love of humanity, learning, and being honored, I mean to ask the following: to what extent are these three traits either the *cause* of other leadership traits or the *foundation* for them to be developed? Our starting point is Xenophon's summary statement of Cyrus' character where he says that Cyrus loved being honored so much that he would "undertake all risks and undergo all dangers for the sake of being praised" (1.2.1). Here I am interested to see where this relationship may apply for other derivative traits and to pin down as carefully as possible the nature of the association.

Before we begin, we must acknowledge two methodological difficulties with arguing that one leadership trait is "fundamental" while another is "derivative." The first is a problem we discussed in the Introduction, that is, we are asking questions that Xenophon may not explicitly answer. With few exceptions, such as *philoponia* (the love of labor), Xenophon does not say that one quality of Cyrus *causes*, or paves the way, for another character trait. Thus, for us to assert that this causality exists will be speculative. It may seem overly simplistic or reductive, as though we are attributing undue sophistication to Xenophon as a leadership theorist, a sophistication that some scholars may be willing to claim while others may not. A way around this problem is to look at other works of Xenophon, or in some cases other Greek authors, where the association is made a more explicit. Another approach is to compare scenes in the *Cyropaedia* to discover either habitual associations or pointed antitheses (as in the case of Cyrus' leadership and that of his uncle, Cyaxares). We will see many places where one fundamental characteristic is regularly *associated with* what I am calling a "derivative" trait. It will be our challenge to clarify this association.

A second problem we face is one of definition. It may be the case that we have defined Cyrus' *philanthrôpia,* etc., in such broad terms that they become, of logical necessity, the "foundation" of plenty of other traits. For example, Cyrus' *philanthrôpia* might seem to subsume justice or gentleness. We even said as much when we said that Cyrus' gentleness was part of his *philanthrôpia* in Chapter One (p. 23). We must be more careful here and guard against this tendency; we will endeavor in this chapter to clarify further what Xenophon means by gentleness (*praotês*). From here we may determine whether it is caused by, subsumed under, or otherwise distinct from his "love of humanity." In the end, whether we call it a "derivative" trait or just another "facet" of Cyrus' *philanthrôpia* is to some extent academic. The ultimate goal is to determine how good Xenophon's Theory of Leadership is vis-à-vis Cyrus' character.

Love of Toil

We have noted that for Xenophon the desire to be honored results in a willingness, if not a desire, to work hard. On the face of it, this correlation is obvious: those who want something will work for it. But to what kinds of work is Xenophon referring? How exactly does work lead to honor and successful leadership?

In his study of *ponos* ("toil") and *ergon* ("work") in Xenophon's *Cynegeticus* and *Oeconomicus*, Johnstone argues that Xenophon was interested in constructing "a style of living, which would justify and enhance the power of elites."[1] For Johnstone *ponos* was an aristocratic and thus highly politicized value that marked out virtuous, practical, and aesthetically pleasing activity, such as hunting and overseeing an estate.[2] Johnstone sees the rise in the idealization of *ponos* in fourth-century Athens as a result of a decline in other social forms of aristocratic distinction, such as luxurious dress, private benefaction to the lower classes, and emphasis on aristocratic lineage, all of which were falling out of favor in Xenophon's time because of the rise of democratic ideology. His remarks about the class significance of *ponos* capture well his position:

> Xenophon sought to define the aristocrat by his toils. Far from being opposed to toil, leisure ... made toil possible. Toil was the stylized, even ostentatious, version of aristocratic leisure, aesthetically and morally superior to the compulsory work of the ordinary person. The labour of the aristocrat was καλός, noble, beautiful, and it won for him virtue. These virtuous practices were concerned not just with the formation of the self ... but essentially with the self as a member of a superior class. Through practices which denied pleasure and asserted self-control, elites would not only distinguish themselves from the populace, but

---

[1] Johnstone 2010:137.
[2] For the role of this ideal in the founders of the American Constitution, see Wulf 2011.

(so Xenophon hoped) moderate their own desires so as to control their competitive urges. Xenophon sought to guarantee the superiority of elites by reforming their culture.

Johnstone 2010:166

Johnstone's characterization of *ponos* in the fourth century is no doubt true to some extent, but it is not entirely true for Xenophon's Cyrus. Yes, *ponos* contributes to the leader's (or the aristocrat's) legitimacy. Leaders need to excel in toil because it will impress their followers, as Cambyses explains to Cyrus:

> On campaigns, if they are in the summer, the leader must *show* that he can overcome the sun; and in the winter, the cold. If he goes through difficult paths, he must *show* he can overcome the toils. For all these things are conducive to his being loved by his followers.

Cyropaedia 1.6.25

And, as we saw in the last chapter, Cambyses emphasizes the mental aspect of toil:

> You must understand this very well, that all the men you should count on to obey you, will count on you to take thought on their behalf. So don't ever be careless, but during the night plan out what your followers will do when the day arrives and during the day plan out how the affairs of the night will be best.

Cyropaedia 1.6.42

This second example again illustrates the social importance of toil: followers expect it of their leaders (cf. *Agesilaus* 5.3). But Cambyses is also emphasizing toil as a practical necessity: leaders have to be responsible for and attentive *to more things* than their followers. Cyrus explains to his father that whereas the Medes think a ruler should surpass the followers in all manner of luxury and sleep, he believes that the ruler should excel others in forethought and enthusiasm for toil (1.6.8). He does not seem to be speaking strictly of ostentatious *toil* here any more than he could be speaking of ostentatious *forethought*.[3] Xenophon's Agesilaus seems to have thoroughly internalized this responsibility:

> Through his activity he employed sleep not as his master but as his follower and, as far as his bed was concerned, if he did not have the

---

[3] For examples of the leader's greater burden of concern elsewhere in Greek literature see Chapter Four pp. 94–96.

most insignificant one of all his comrades, he could not conceal his shame. *For he thought that a leader should not surpass private citizens in softness but in endurance (karteria).*

Agesilaus 5.2

Xenophon's Cyrus conceives of toil as a means to prosperity both for leaders and followers, not as an end in itself or as a means to legitimacy. He explains to his men as they divide up the spoils of conquest:

Hereafter, too, we must be good men, knowing that obedience, endurance, and toil and danger in the opportune moment provide great pleasures and great benefits.

Cyropaedia 3.3.8

Besides being necessary for success, toil is demanding, dirty, and unglamorous. Persian youths endure heat and cold on the hunt as well as deprivation of food and water (1.2.10–11). In the *Anabasis*, Cyrus the Younger orders Persian nobles to dislodge some wagons from the mud, which they do in all haste while wearing their fancy clothes and jewelry. This exercise was, says Xenophon, an example of their discipline and orderliness (1.5.7–8). Xenophon himself chops wood in the snow, without a cloak, to inspire similar toil and endurance in his men (4.4.12).

A priori it may seem that a leader could only engage in stylized labor or exhibitions of hard labor that are obviously staged. Where would the leader find the energy to do more than others? Cambyses explains to Cyrus how it is conceivable that a leader might actually be able to labor more than the followers:

Understand that *though they have the same kinds of bodies*, these toils do not affect the man who is a leader as the private citizen, but the position of honor (*tîmê*) and the very knowledge that whatever he should do does not lie hidden lessens the toils for the leader somewhat.

Cyropaedia 1.6.25

It follows, then, that a leader with a superlative love of being honored would be able to endure and toil in all sorts of ways to win the respect of the followers.[4] While it is conceivable that the followers might be impressed by elite forms of

---

[4] Xenophon's Agesilaus seems to have had something of this principle in mind when he made it a policy never to sleep in a private house when he traveled but rather in a temple (where the gods would be watching) or in a public place where everyone could witness his *sôphrosunê* (*Agesilaus* 5.7). As we have already seen, Cyrus is very adept at preempting what would be considered less

toil that they are excluded from participating in, it is equally true for Xenophon that extra toil is required for the leader and that the leader must win the respect of the followers by competing with them in the same kinds of (menial) labor that they might routinely perform.

Self-mastery, Self-restraint, and Endurance

Do *philanthrôpia*, *philomatheia*, and *philotîmia* somehow lead to a more restrained leader? In Xenophon, self-mastery (*enkrateia*) typically refers to a control over physical distractions, e.g. food, drink, hot, cold, and sleep, whereas self-restraint (*sôphrosunê*) refers to emotional distractions, with fear, anger, pity, and love being among the most potent. We may think of self-restraint and mastery as complements of *philoponia*, in the sense that they involve the strength *not* to engage in certain actions.

For Cyrus, self-restraint is learned in the Persian educational system and is thus presumably teachable. Youths learn self-restraint by observing their elders carry on in a moderate way (1.2.8). Accordingly, a good student should be able to learn it, the exceptional student even more so. Interestingly, so should a good teacher: Xenophon says that Cyrus became most accomplished at "self-mastery and the arts of exercise and war" by engaging in training his comrades (8.1.37). Insofar as restraint is something done in a public setting, we would expect the lover of honor to be able to possess more of it than others, just as he or she will toil more than others. As we observed above, the spotlight that shines on the leader lightens the burden; perhaps Xenophon means to imply that the same is true of restraint.

This is probably as far as we may go in drawing connections to Cyrus' *philotîmia*, unless we assume that when Xenophon speaks of *ponos*, he means to include *all forms* of physical effort, from restraint to endurance to positive exertion. Finally, in pointing out a correlation between these traits, I am not saying that *philotîmia* is the *only* basis for becoming restrained. Xenophon has the stern Persian soldier Aglaïtadas explain that fathers teach sons self-restraint by making them cry, presumably by inducing fear (2.2.14). Tigranes argues, too, that someone can learn self-restraint through fear: his own father, he says, has learned to restrain himself first by being defeated in battle by Cyrus, the superior general, and then by being threatened with death (3.1.16-23). As we noted in the Introduction, Plato argues that an intense love of otherworldly wisdom

---

than virtuous behavior, e.g. when he refuses to gaze on Pantheia or when he checks his greedy impulse by distributing his wealth to friends (Chapter Two pp. 55–56).

(*philosophia*) also renders someone restrained against the pleasures and experiences of the corporeal world (see Introduction pp. 12–13).

Justice

Xenophon says that Persians learn justice (*dikaiosunê*) in their educational system in the same way that Greeks learn their alphabet (1.2.6). To become proficient in this trait, boys play the part of prosecutors and judges, bringing charges against one another and passing sentence according to the offense. They are particularly keen to prosecute acts of ingratitude, which they see as a path to shamefulness. Xenophon says that Cyrus excels all others in learning his lessons in justice or otherwise, because he learns so quickly. The ability to become a just person is teachable and thus derives at least in part from Cyrus' love of learning.

But this does not seem to be the entire picture. In Plato, the Philosopher King is also said to be proficient in justice, not only because of his intelligence but because of his love of otherworldly wisdom. As we noted in the Introduction, Plato's lover of wisdom does not care about material possessions and thus would not be interested in cheating others of them (pp. 12–13). Justice is each person doing his or her part according to what is fitting for the community. The implication is that as long as the Philosopher King is benefitting the community (and not seeking personal gain), then it is appropriate to apply the notion of what is fitting or just without consideration for what others believe or feel. This lack of consideration goes as far as fabricating "noble lies" like the Myth of Metals, wherein members of the community are instructed to let the rearing of children take place according to a pairing of the most suitable children with the most suitable parents (*Republic* 415a–c). This level of deception is not occasional, but chronic in a community where (it is assumed) some members are leaders and some are not, some may understand the true reason behind a political decision and others may never be capable of comprehending it.

Xenophon's Cyrus does use deception at times, even to benefit his friends, just as the Philosopher King does, but typically his deception is temporary.[5] As a young man, he administers justice without considering the feelings of those under him, for example, when he judges the case of the two boys and their coats (1.3.16–18). In this scene a larger boy takes a large coat from a smaller boy and then gives his own small coat in return. Cyrus approves. On a logical level, this solution seems fitting, even a good example of "philanthropic" match-making; the interests of one party are paired with those of another into an objectively

---

[5]   Cf. Danzig (forthcoming):13–17 on Cyrus' benevolent deception of his uncle Cyaxares.

harmonious arrangement. The young Cyrus is punished, however, for failing to recognize that justice requires doing what is *lawful* in regard to the two coats. Cyrus learns that Persian children have what we might call "property rights" to their clothes that cannot be transgressed by coercion simply because a judge deems it beneficial to the two of them to do so. Cyrus explains to his mother that he has learned the distinction between what is fitting (*to harmotôn*) and what is lawful (*to nomimon*), such as the ownership of something made or purchased.[6] Injustice in this scene is called "*biaion*" (coercive), which, as Danzig points out, Xenophon uses to apply "to every unlawful act … in opposition to persuasion as meaning 'perpetrated against someone's will'."[7]

Cyrus seems to have learned from his incomplete understanding of justice when he proposes the alliance of land-sharing between the Armenians and Chaldaeans. We may think of this scene as the counterpart to the Two Coats story. Here Cyrus carefully asks permission from both parties before confirming the treaty (3.2.17–24). To the Chaldaeans he says:

> Would you like the opportunity to cultivate the Armenian land, as much of it as you wanted, on the condition that you pay as much as other Armenians?

When the Chaldaeans agree, Cyrus asks the Armenian king if he would be willing to let the Chaldaeans cultivate the untended land, to which he agrees. In reciprocal terms, he then requests a similar consent from the Chaldaeans to allow the Armenians to pasture their herds in their mountains—and then asks if this arrangement is agreeable to the Armenians. Nevertheless, the Chaldaeans and Armenians both stipulate that the mountains adjoining their two lands should not be occupied by either side (as they would feel mutually threatened), but that Cyrus should place a garrison there. Both sides then give their approval of the treaty. Both sides are then enthusiastic to build the fort for their common safety. Xenophon points out that the two nations shared the right of intermarriage and that the covenant is still intact in his day.

By the end of the episode it is clear that although Cyrus has the authority and means to compel the Armenians and Chaldaeans to accept a "fitting" arrangement, he creates an environment where the wishes (and property) of both sides are respected, even to the point of allowing each side to make their own emendations to the treaty. Justice, then, seems to require a consideration for the rights and feelings of those to whom it is administered. It is a function of

---

[6] On the similarity to this scene and Socrates' discussions of justice in the *Memorabilia*, see Gera 1993:74–75.
[7] Danzig 2010:278–279.

Cyrus' love of learning as well as his fondness for others, particularly his ability to share in their good fortune and in their sorrows.[8]

Again we see similar consideration when Cyrus plans to reward his comrades according to their performance in battle; here, too, he asks for their approval (2.3.4). Pheraulas approves of Cyrus as the distributor of the spoils because Cyrus is free from envy and takes more pleasure in benefiting others than himself (2.3.12). When Cyrus and his men have acquired spoils in their pursuit of the Assyrians, he insists that they wait for their allies to return in order to divide them fairly. Moreover, he insists that the allies be their own arbiters in the distribution, with mutual good will being the basis of their trust that the process will be fair (4.2.42, 4.5.44–45).

In short, justice for Cyrus is not simply about knowing what is fitting but also caring about the feelings and interests of others. It has an intellectual and sympathetic component; part of being fair is the *desire* to be fair. Indeed, Xenophon seems to agree with Aristotle, who says that just individuals need to have friendly feeling toward one another and that intense friendliness is characteristic of the just (*Nicomachean Ethics* 1155a26–28).

Gentleness

Whereas *philanthrôpia* is a fondness for others and a desire to help them, it has we might call a complement in the form of *praotês* ("gentleness" or "mildness"), the practice of *not harming others* in situations where harshness or violence might be expected. *Praotês* in a leadership context is the tendency not to retaliate when contradicted, rivaled, threatened, or betrayed. In particular, it often entails not becoming envious, though leaders have abundant opportunities to do so. For example, Pindar portrays Hieron, the tyrant of Syracuse, as "gentle to his citizens, not envious of good men, and a wondrous father to foreign guests."[9] Agesilaus is gentle for not treating his captives as criminals, and his gentleness blends into his practice of *philanthrôpia* to the point that they seem synonymous (*Agesilaus* 1.21–22). Aristotle says that the tyrant Pisistratus was "philanthropic" and gentle, as well as understanding toward those who committed an offense against him.[10] Pisistratus was both a "man of the people" (*dêmotikos*)

---

[8] Cf. Konstan 2007:216. On the Persian king's reputation for justice in Greek culture, cf. Hirsh 1985:7–8.

[9] Cf. πραΰς ἀστοῖς, οὐ φθονέων ἀγαθοῖς, ξεί-| νοις δὲ θαυμαστὸς πατήρ, *Pythian Odes* 3.71–72. Cf. the gentle words and hospitality of the would-be king, Jason (μειλιχίοισι λόγοις, *Pythian Odes* 4.127).

[10] Cf. φιλάνθρωπος ἦν καὶ πρᾷος καὶ τοῖς ἁμαρτάνουσι συγγνωμονικός, *Athenian Constitution* 16.2.4. Pisitratus' *philanthrôpia* was manifested in the loans he made to poorer farmers; his motive, according to Aristotle, does not seem to have been to improve the well-being of the poorer Athenians *per se*, so much as to keep them out of the city and thus out of politics.

and "philanthropic" for his obedience to the laws and willingness to stand trial (*Athenian Constitution* 16.8.3). The Cyprian king, Nicocles, boasts of his gentleness: "toward the citizens of the state I behaved with such mildness (*praotês*) that no one has suffered exile or death or confiscation of property or any such misfortune during my reign" (Isocrates *Nicocles* 32.4–8).

Cyrus exhibits some of the behavior toward his enemies that characterized Agesilaus' gentleness (*Cyropaedia* 4.4.6–7). The Armenian nobles marvel at his gentleness in not recklessly punishing the Armenian king for refusing to pay tribute and plotting rebellion (cf. τὴν πρᾳότητα, 3.1.41.2; cf. 3.1.9.5). Instead, Cyrus patiently listens to Tigranes' plea on his father's behalf, questioning him until Tigranes convinces Cyrus that the Armenian king no longer poses a threat and could be a valuable ally.[11] Cyrus is also praised as gentle and understanding for not punishing Araspas for falling in love with the captive Pantheia (cf. πρᾷός τε καὶ συγγνώμων, 6.1.37.3).

Even when Cyrus is not called "gentle," his actions may be seen as such, in the sense that they demonstrate a mild disposition or the absence of envy (*phthonos*) when envy might be expected. Whereas Cyrus' uncle, Cyaxares, behaves harshly toward those who are disobedient in pursuit of honor (see below), Cyrus shows understanding for the brave Cadusian prince who recklessly pursues the Assyrians (5.4.19). As we noted in Chapter One (p. 23), the boy Cyrus challenges his Medan contemporaries to contests of horseback riding, knowing that he will lose and even laughing at himself, to the delight of others (1.4.9–17). When Cyrus goes hunting, his grandfather forbids anyone to cast a spear before Cyrus does, but the youth insists that each of his comrades be allowed to compete according to the best of his ability (1.4.14). During the hunt Astyages delights in the fact that Cyrus praises his comrades without a modicum of envy.[12] In public assemblies Cyrus takes counsel with others, solicits counter-proposals, and even adopts them contrary to his own proposal.[13] The only character Cyrus shows a lack of gentleness toward is the cupbearer, Sacas, who thwarts the young Cyrus' visits to his grandfather.[14] Eventually, Cyrus wins the freedom to visit his grandfather whenever he likes and even takes Sacas on as a friendly advisor, so that the cupbearer becomes exceedingly fond of Cyrus (1.4.6.9).

---

[11] *Cyropaedia* 3.1.9.5. Cyrus also rewards the gentleness of one taxiarch (2.3.21.15). This is only the third instance of the noun, *praotês*, in Xenophon; the two others describe Agesilaus and Cyrus.

[12] Cf. οὐδ' ὁπωστιοῦν φθονερῶς, 1.4.15.7. Cf. Cyrus as one who judges without envy (2.3.12.3, 3.2.28.7).

[13] *Cyropaedia* 4.5.24, 6.2.24, 6.2.39, 6.3.36, 6.4.19, 7.5.7, 7.5.37, 8.3.2. Plato also praises this feature of Cyrus' non-envious leadership (*Laws* 694b).

[14] *Cyropaedia* 1.3.8–11. In presenting this rivalry with Sacas, Xenophon may be alluding to an alternate version of Cyrus' rise to power as the faithful cupbearer of Astyages (Cook 26).

Contrary to Cyrus' gentleness, the Armenian king envies Tigranes' tutor (3.1.39) and the Assyrian king is murderously envious of his peers. After inviting the son of Gobryas on a hunting expedition, the Assyrian king is plagued with envy because the young man surpasses him by bringing down both a bear and a lion (cf. τὸν φθόνον, 4.6.4.1, 4.6.4.8). As a result, he impulsively kills him. The king's father expresses sympathy for Gobryas' misfortune (4.6.5.7), but his son shows no sympathy; neither does he try to make amends nor does he honor Gobryas' son. Later, he has the noble Gadatas made into a eunuch because one of his concubines praised Gadatas' beauty (5.2.28).

Cyrus' uncle, Cyaxares, is also sensitive to rivalry, though he commits none of the same acts of outrage as the Assyrian king. After Cyrus pursues the Assyrians with a band of Cyaxeres' own Medan troops, Cyaxares exhibits harshness (ômotês) because he feels abandoned and left out of the larger campaign. In his fury he orders a message to be delivered to Cyrus immediately, an act that Xenophon describes as consistent with his harshness and lack of understanding (cf. ὠμὸς ... καὶ ἀγνώμων, 4.5.9.6). Xenophon points out that such harshness can be anathema to the leader's goal of winning the followers' willing obedience.[15]

Given this prominent antithesis between the harsh envy of others and Cyrus' own gentleness, we should attempt to pin down the association between gentleness and *philanthrôpia* more carefully. It would be hasty and oversimplified to conclude that *philanthrôpia* is the source of all forms of gentleness in a leader, however. *A priori* we could imagine several reasons why a leader might feel or show *praotês*: self-confidence, confidence that any rivals are too weak or fear-stricken to offer a viable threat, a personal desire for self-improvement through competition, a sense of fairness, the capacity to understand another's perspective, or, finally, a fondness for others and the desire to benefit them directly (*philanthrôpia*). Many of these explanations would work for the examples we have seen in the *Cyropaedia*. Cyrus might be willing to compete with (and lose to) his age-mates at horseback riding because he knows it will help him improve (1.3.15). He might be willing to compete more formally in the horse race he himself sponsors in Babylon because he believes no one would dare to challenge him (8.3.25). He might be willing for his comrades to compete equally in the hunt because he is confident that he will be the best; if so, he is right. He might be willing to listen to counter-proposals from his men because he already enjoys their good will and is confident in his own ability to give sensible advice. He might be willing to listen to the plea of Tigranes for the Armenian king or to pardon Araspas' advances on Pantheia because he has the intelligence

---

15   Cf. τὴν ὠμότητα, 4.5.19.4. The usage of *omotês* to describe Cyaxares here is the only occurrence in Xenophon, though the Spartan commander Clearchus is similarly harsh and has a similarly hard time commanding the obedience of his followers (cf. ἀεὶ χαλεπὸς ἦν καὶ ὠμός, *Anabasis* 2.6.12.3).

and empathy to take their perspectives and to comprehend the rationale for their behavior.[16] We could say that whereas Cyaxares is harsh and lacking in understanding (ὠμὸς καὶ ἀγνώμων), Cyrus is gentle and understanding (πρᾷός καὶ συγγνώμων). As we noted above, Persians are trained in the virtue of justice as part of their education system; in particular they are trained to hear cases and pass judgment on them (1.2.6). So, where does *philanthrôpia* figure into this picture?

Rather than being instinctual or natural, Cyrus' *praotês* may involve some calculation, or at least may be part of a larger network of considerations. For example, in the case of his gentleness toward the Armenians (i.e. patiently listening to Tigranes' defense of his father), Cyrus sets out to gain tribute from the Armenians; on top of that, he ends up controlling their entire army (2.4.12, 3.1.42). To punish the Armenians might be just, but their services as allies are of greater advantage. Similarly, by showing gentleness and understanding to Araspas Cyrus can use him as a spy on the Assyrians (6.1.39). In competition, whether hunting or riding, Cyrus' gentleness wins him the affection and later the allegiance of his Medan friends.

Thus, in showing gentleness, Cyrus seems to pursue a specific policy of leadership: he establishes his authority as a leader on the formation of loyal friendships (cf. his advice to his sons at *Cyropaedia* 8.7.13). This policy is an explicit part of Cyrus' practice of "showing" his *philanthrôpia* (cf. 8.2.1). Cyrus is renowned for saying that a king is like a shepherd because both must know how to benefit their "flocks" in order to draw benefits in return (8.2.14). We might imagine that leaders could follow this policy whether or not they had an intrinsic desire to help others, but it would be easier for leaders to implement it if they took direct pleasure in helping others, as Cyrus does.[17] Thus we may conclude that while Xenophon may not mean to say that *philanthrôpia* is the *only* cause of Cyrus' *praotês*, it can be the basic trait that makes it easier for a leader to implement a policy of authority based on friendship.

Attentiveness

In the previous Chapter, when I noted Cyrus' eagerness to learn about military affairs, I suggested that *philomatheia* and *epimeleia* were nearly synonymous, or that *epimeleia* was the activity that a *philomathês* tends to engage in. In the *Oeconomicus*, Xenophon explains that *epimeleia* is an important virtue that may

---

[16] In praising Cyrus' *praotês* the Armenians also praise his wisdom (*sophia*) (3.1.41).

[17] Danzig (forthcoming):8–9 makes the valuable point that Cyrus learns from his father that the best way to appear to be something is actually to be it. Thus we could infer the same for *philanthrôpia*: the best way to base one's legitimacy as a leader on friendship is to enjoy making friends.

be taught. Ischomachus explains to Socrates how it is that he teaches the overseers of his estate to be good at what they do (12.5). Both speakers acknowledge that it is not enough for the overseer to be loyal and well-meaning, and so Ischomachus explains that he also teaches attentiveness (*epimeleia*). Socrates doubts that anyone can be taught to be attentive, but Ischomachus says that it takes a certain kind of student. Those who are vulnerable to alcohol or sleep, he says, cannot be taught, as well as those who are desperately in love (i.e. those with minimal self-restraint and self-mastery). When Socrates doubts if the greedy would be good candidates to learn, Ischomachus claims that they are, as long as it is explained to them that attentiveness is profitable, though he acknowledges that such people are dangerous. Finally, Socrates asks how he teaches the person who is only a moderate lover of gain and free from other faults, to which Ischomachus replies:

> Very easily, Socrates. For whenever I notice them being attentive, I both praise them and try to honor them, but whenever they are careless, I try to say or do whatever will sting them.

Oeconomicus 12.16

Ischomachus says further that he prefers lovers of honor to lovers of gain (*philokerdeis*). He prefers a man who is honest not only because it is profitable but because an honest man is eager for praise from him; the ambitious (*philotîmoi*), he says, are willing to toil however it is necessary, to take risks, and refrain from shameful gain (14.10). Ischomachus does not make the deduction, but he implies that the person who is highly loving of honor would also be highly attentive, assuming such a person saw opportunities to win honor by doing so. *philomatheia* and *philotîmia*, then, seem to work together to enhance *epimeleia*.

Piety

Piety is neither a virtue that boys study in the Persian *agôgê* nor is it part of Cyrus' education at the court of his grandfather. Plutarch does say that the later Persian king, Artaxerxes II, learned the skill of the Magi from a priest who had been appointed to give him the traditional Persian education (*Life of Artaxerxes* 3.3). But Xenophon mentions neither the gods nor their worship until well into Chapter Five of Book One of the *Cyropaedia*. There he says that Cyrus, having selected his Persian comrades to join Cyaxares in his war against the Assyrians, consults the gods and does not march out until the omens were favorable (1.5.6). As a conclusion to his speech exhorting his men to fight with confidence, he assures them that he has not been inattentive to the gods (1.5.14). Though there has been no mention of this practice thus far, he claims to have always set out with approval from the gods in matters both great and small.

From this point in the work Xenophon's attention to religion picks up considerably. After his speech Cyrus goes home to pray to ancestral Hestia and Zeus as well as the other gods, from whom he receives the favorable omen of thunder and lightning (1.6.1). Gera gives a thorough and thoughtful account of this religiosity in the *Cyropaedia*, which I briefly summarize here.[18] Religion is given prominence in Cyrus' lengthy dialogue with Cambyses in that it both begins and ends with auspicious omens. Cambyses tells Cyrus that it is important for him to learn the art of soothsaying himself, lest he be dependent on others who might trick him or otherwise be unavailable. Cambyses stresses that nothing should be done without divine approval and that the gods should be remembered especially in times of prosperity. Gera points out that this need for the future king to be familiar with rituals, sacrifices, and omens, may derive from Xenophon's understanding of the Persian king's traditional role in such activity. Xenophon does not go much further in explaining Persian religion, however, saying nothing about the early Achaemenids and Zoroastrianism. Cyrus does utilize the Magi in determining which gods should receive what spoils and he somehow reforms their order (8.1.23).

Gera notes that Cyrus carries out all of his father's instructions throughout his campaign, but she finds Xenophon's treatment of Cyrus' religion disappointing: "despite Cyrus' outstanding piety ... religion in the *Cyropaedia* is not the living, motive factor that it is, for example, in the *Anabasis*."[19] By "motive factor" Gera means that dreams, omens, and signs do not play an important role in advancing the plot of the *Cyropaedia*.[20] Cyrus always receives good omens and all sacrifices turn out favorably, making his consultation of them "mechanical" and their approval "automatic."[21] We could go further and say that clever interpretation plays very little role in worshipping the gods: there is no responsibility to figure out, for example, what "wooden walls" or "destroying a mighty empire" might mean, as in so often the case in Herodotus' *Histories*. Gera speculates that Xenophon may not have wanted Cyrus to face challenges from the gods, or that Xenophon's view of religion had become more "routine and unthinking over the years."[22] Ultimately, Gera declares that religion in the *Cyropaedia* itself seems "routine and unthinking."[23]

[18] Gera 1993:54–59.
[19] Gera 1993:58.
[20] The one exception is the dream Cyrus receives at the end of his life that foretells his death (8.7.2).
[21] Gera 1993:59.
[22] Gera 1993:59.
[23] Gera 1993:284.

Gera is correct to point out the mechanical nature of Xenophon's portrayal of Cyrus' piety; it does not "enliven" the work much, at least from a dramatic perspective. Yet, I think the explanation lies not in Xenophon's desire to minimize conflict or his lack of interest in religion, but rather in his focus on the leader's attentiveness (*epimeleia*) and self-restraint. To the extent that attentiveness seems prosaic, so does Cyrus' piety, but it is still crucial to his success as a leader. As Cambyses explains to Cyrus, people who have on all occasions shown attention to the gods (*epimeleiai*) and not neglected them can more confidently expect their prayers to be answered (1.6.4–5). A particularly good example of Cyrus' thoroughness in matters of religion may be found on the eve of his invasion of Assyria. Before entering the country, he sacrifices to Zeus "the King" and the other gods, and he calls for help from the Medan heroes. Once in enemy country, he makes offerings to Gaia and sacrifices to the gods and heroes of the Assyrians. He sacrifices again to Zeus of his Fatherland and "neglects none of the other divinities" that were brought to his attention.[24]

Moreover, knowledge of religion for Xenophon, it would seem, is much like knowledge of farming, in that the information is readily available and comparatively unambiguous. Yet, few individuals make the effort to apply such knowledge vigilantly on all occasions. Often some character flaw gets in the way: for example, Herodotus' Croesus is told that by invading the Persians he will destroy a mighty empire. As the oracle later explains to him, he had the opportunity to ask which empire he would destroy, but he neglected to, presumably because he was overconfident (*Histories* 1.19). In the *Cyropaedia*, Cyrus feels a similar temptation at the beginnings of his battles to presume favor from the gods, or to look for favor where there is none. Yet Xenophon has him check his impulses and pay attention.

Specifically, Xenophon has Cyrus trained to check himself in times of prosperity.[25] His father emphasizes this in their lengthy conversation (1.6.3), and Cyrus regularly consults with the Magi on what to offer the gods. As we noted earlier, at the end of his life he is grateful for the fact that he never became excessively joyous in life because he always anticipated that something troubling might happen to him (Chapter Two, p. 56). In language that sharply contrasts with the mistakes of Herodotus' Cyrus (who had entertained immortal thoughts), Cyrus expresses his gratitude to the gods that he always recognized their attentive care and never thought "more than human thoughts" in his good fortune (cf. οὐδεπώποτε ... ὑπὲρ ἄνθρωπον ἐφρόνησα, 8.7.3). It is this kind of

---

[24] *Cyropaedia* 3.3.21–22. Cyrus is as mindful of what he owes to his fatherland as to the gods (4.5.17).
[25] For this theme in the *Hellenica*, see Dillery 1995:242.

restraint in prosperity that wins the Assyrian Gobryas' respect for the Persians and his willingness to marry his daughter to one of them (8.4.14).

So, on one level, we may say that piety is not so much caused by or grounded in a love of learning (or attentiveness); it is a *kind* of attentiveness to what the gods want and what they intend. But piety for Xenophon is also about abiding by one's oaths and may be seen as a consequence of the fact that the gods know more than humans: since they know more, they know when humans are breaking their oaths.[26] In his encomium to Agesilaus, Xenophon explains that the Spartan king was able to gain the upper (moral) hand against his rival, the Persian satrap, Tissaphernes, by abiding by the agreement they had called upon the gods to witness (*Agesilaus* 1.9.12). On other occasions Agesilaus was able to stand as a guarantor of oaths among others (3.2–5). For his part, Cyrus forms an alliance with the Assyrian Gobryas by a pledge of right hands and by calling upon the gods as witnesses (4.6.10). Later, after Cyrus has shown his willingness to help Gobryas avenge the murder of his son, Gobryas publicly praises Cyrus' faithfulness (6.1.11). Finally, after Cyrus dies, Xenophon offers his analysis of the fall of the Persian Empire, beginning with their neglect of the gods. Whereas in the past Persians had won a good reputation by upholding their oaths (even among their worst enemies), now in their degeneration no one trusts them (8.8.2–3). Xenophon is particularly rueful of the perfidy of Artaxerxes II, by whom he had been betrayed in his expedition with Cyrus the Younger.

This emphasis on obedience to oaths sworn before the eyes of the gods could be characterized as a function of the leader's love of honor, justice,[27] a concern for others, or a mindfulness or fear of retribution from the gods. In short, Xenophon implies that a leader who loves humanity, learning, and being honored will likely be mindful of what the gods want, how to appease them, and why it's always a good idea to abide by oaths.

The Aesthetics of Leadership

The love of beauty is a character trait that appears early in the *Cyropaedia* and then sporadically, but its importance resonates throughout the work. When Cyrus arrives in Media, his grandfather dresses him in the traditional Medan style and teaches him to ride, which Xenophon says he delights in doing because he is a lover of beauty (*philokalos*) and a lover of honor (1.3.2). What is beautiful (*kalos*) is often easily recognized as that which is expensive or fancy. In

---

[26] For the importance of abiding by one's oaths in the *Memorabilia* and *Hellenica*, cf. Dillery 1995:183–185.

[27] In his discussion of Persian decline, Xenophon specifically links the good reputation (*doxa*) to be had with piety and associates impiety (*asebeia*) with injustice (*adikia*) (8.8.2–7).

battle Cyrus wears the finest armor (1.4.18, 7.1.2, cf. Abradatas, 6.4.1–4). When he comes to rule Babylon, he instructs his associates to adopt the Medan style of dress, with eyeliner and elevated shoes, in order to make themselves more distinguished and thus charm their subjects (8.1.40–41).

What qualifies as beautiful can be subjective, however, at least on the visual level. When asked who is more beautiful, his father or grandfather, Cyrus politely explains that they are both "most beautiful" in their respective cultures, Cambyses among the more modestly dressed Persians and Astyages among the luxurious Medes (1.3.2). On his campaign against the Assyrians, Cyrus is summoned by Cyaxares to marshal his troops to greet an envoy of Indians. Rather than put on their full armor and finery, Cyrus has them form their ranks and march as quickly as possible to join the envoy. When Cyaxares censures him for not appearing as radiant and magnificent as possible (λαμπρότατον, μεγαλοπρεπέστατον), Cyrus contends that being "adorned" (κεκοσμημένος) with sweat and haste are a greater mark of honor to Cyaxares (2.4.5–6). When Cyrus himself is in the leadership role, he feels that his beauty is reflected in the fine possessions and clothes of his followers, a commonplace sentiment in Xenophon.[28] When he marries, Cyrus' wife's reputation for beauty is the trait that most recommends her (8.5.28).

To get a better sense of the foundations of the love of beauty, we may consider other places where the term is used in Xenophon. For one, Cyrus on campaign sets up a series of contests among the different classes of soldier, beginning with the private, whom he says must excel in several different qualities:

ἰδιώτῃ μὲν ἑαυτὸν παρέχειν εὐπειθῆ τοῖς ἄρχουσι καὶ ἐθελόπονον καὶ φιλοκίνδυνον μετ᾽ εὐταξίας καὶ ἐπιστήμονα τῶν στρατιωτικῶν καὶ <u>φιλόκαλον περὶ ὅπλα</u> καὶ φιλότιμον ἐπὶ πᾶσι τοῖς τοιούτοις.

The private must show himself obedient to his commanding officers, ready to work, eager to take risks in good order, knowledgeable of tactics, *a lover of beauty in regard to his armor*, and a lover of being honored in all these respects.[29]

Cyropaedia 2.1.22

---

[28] *Cyropaedia* 3.3.6, 8.3.4; cf. *Anabasis* 1.9.23, *Hieron* 11.2.1.

[29] Though I am not focusing on what Xenophon calls Cyrus' one superlative physical trait, beauty (*Cyropaedia* 1.2.1), it is interesting to note that Critobulus in Xenophon's *Symposium* argues that a beautiful general would be capable of making his followers more "lovers of toil" and "lovers of beauty" in dangerous situations (4.15). Cyrus' beauty may partly explain his effect on his followers here.

Later, when he defeats Croesus in battle, Cyrus incorporates him into his army after he sees the Lydians "priding themselves in the adornment" of their weapons, horses, and chariots.[30] As we saw in the boy Cyrus and his fine clothes, we again see an association of the love of beauty with the love of honor. It would seem then that at least part of what it means to "love beauty" for Xenophon is to love being honored for one's visual distinctiveness, that is, to be recognized as the visual embodiment of certain honorable virtues, such as promptness, restraint, or diligence.

In addition to being an expression of honor, the love of beauty also seems to be tied to the intellectual virtue of good order or arrangement (*eutaxis*).[31] When Cyrus decides that he would like to set up an elaborate procession through Babylon, he tasks the Persian commoner Pheraulas to help him devise a parade that will be both beautiful to those who were benevolent toward him and also most intimidating to those who were hostile. He chooses Pheraulas for his intelligence, love of beauty, and orderliness (cf. καὶ συνετὸν ... καὶ φιλόκαλον καὶ εὔτακτον, 8.3.5).

Dillery has shown that order is fundamental to Xenophon's worldview, noting several places where it is praised in the household, the army, the *polis*, and beyond.[32] In Chapter Eight of the *Oeconomicus*, Ischomachus praises order (*taxis*) in a chorus of dancers, calling them "ugly to look at" when they perform independently of one another (8.3). He goes on to say that all sorts of things appear more beautiful when they are arranged in order (e.g. sandals, cloaks, and linens). One of the main values of order is that it allows each thing to be used for some good because it is readily accessible. Thus, Ischomachus advises his wife to order their house so that they will know where everything is to be put to use.

Dillery shows that Cyrus, too, favors this love of order as a means to greater efficiency. Cyrus is raised in an educational system that is organized by tribe, age, and merit (1.2.4–16). As a leader, he encourages his subordinates to pick their troops not on the basis of native origin but on the basis of their excellence. He espouses the same general appreciation for order elsewhere in Xenophon: "things that are disorganized (ἀσύντακτα) are always troublesome until they are put in order" (4.5.37). He uses the analogy of a house that is better lacking

---

[30] Cf. καλλωπιζομένους, 7.4.14.2. Xenophon says contemporary Persians shamefully take pride in adorning themselves with as many drinking cups as possible (*Cyropaedia* 8.8.18).

[31] Breebaart 1983:120 notes the form that this "arrangement" takes: "Xenophon was primarily interested in the administrative channeling of monarchical virtue to all subjects. This implies that he had to pay more attention to 'technical' means, allowing the virtues of the commander to reach all subjects, than to the constitutional pattern of the state. The articulation of peacetime monarchy turned on an efficient administrative structure of spreading 'virtue', not on constitutional principles or delimitation of rights."

[32] Dillery 1995:31–35, 252.

in slaves altogether than "disordered" by wicked ones (cf. ταραττόμενος, 2.2.26). He again follows Ischomachus in applying the analogy of the ordered household to the ordered army:

> Cyrus thought that orderliness (*euthêmosunê*) was also a good practice in the household. For whenever someone needed something, it was clear from where it was necessary for him to go and take it. But he thought that orderliness in military groupings was far better.
>
> *Cyropaedia* 8.5.7

Xenophon explains that Cyrus assigned this preeminence to military organization because in war the dangers and chances for success are much greater. At its best, Cyrus' army functions with greater coordination than a chorus, given its exceptional training and obedience to his commands (3.3.70). When his camp is conceived with good organization, it is easier for him to know who is and is not following orders (8.5.14). Outside of the army, Cyrus draws the greatest benefit from orderliness when he applies both the Persian system of education and military organization (*suntaxis*) to his government by dividing everyone into units of ten, with each administrator overseeing ten men below him on down the chain of command (8.1.14).

In his Funeral Oration in the *Histories* of Thucydides, which is the first extant use of the *philokal-* stem, Pericles says of his fellow Athenians, "we are lovers of beauty with a purpose" (Φιλοκαλοῦμέν ... μετ' εὐτελείας, 2.40.1). For Xenophon, and perhaps for Thucydides, the purpose of beauty (or order) was to charm, intimidate, and impress others. It was also a means to efficiency and to facilitate the leader's grasp of a situation, whether an array of troops in battle formation or satraps in imperial administration. We may think of the love of organization that Cyrus shows as a necessary component of his love of learning: since it is important for a leader to have the kind of mind that maintains a hyper-attentiveness to all things, such a leader must also have the proclivity to organize all these data-points into a "beautiful" unity. Here again we see the extent to which the love of learning in Xenophon does not involve brilliance, cleverness, or invention, so much as a careful attention to all that is knowable, from the gods and from friends, guided by an orderly arrangement of the operation and all the information therein.

Conclusion

Cyrus' superlative love of humanity, love of learning, and love of being honored seem conducive to several other traits central to his success as a leader. The love of honor seems to do the most work, giving the leader the motivation to pay more attention, take greater risks, toil harder, endure more, and sacrifice love and other conveniences of the body. In some cases, a derivative trait may arise from the coordination of two fundamental traits: the love of learning and the love of humanity seem to produce a more just and gentle Cyrus; and the love of honor and the love of learning seem to make him more pious and loving of beauty (order).

While these superlative "loves" may be conducive to these other traits, they are not the only cause of them, as we have noted in several places. A leader might behave gently not out of a love for humanity so much as out of self-confidence or out of a desire to *seem* merciful. Similarly, a leader might show restraint not out of a desire to win honor but, according to Plato's Socrates, because the emotions and the pleasures of the body hold no interest compared to understanding the Forms.

As I stressed at the outset of this chapter, such an approach to the fundamentality of Xenophon's Theory of Leadership is of necessity conjectural, and can become reductive and simplistic. With few exceptions (like the love of honor producing the love of toil), Xenophon never says that *philanthrôpia*, etc. are the more fundamental traits. He does say that they are features of Cyrus' soul, and he does repeatedly talk about "derivative" traits in associative ways, both of which facts invite us to explore how Xenophon may have conceived of leadership characteristics in fundamental and derivative ways.

4

Six Problems with Loving Humanity

IT IS ONE THING TO OBSERVE how a leader is portrayed with fundamental and derivative traits; it is still more important to determine how well these traits actually translate into effective leadership. In the next three chapters we consider the implications of Cyrus' *philanthrôpia*, *philomatheia*, and *philotîmia* and their fundamentality for fourteen problems inherent in these characteristics. In doing so, we wrestle with some of the universal problems of leadership, ones that are tied to the problem of how to secure the willing obedience of followers, a central feature of Xenophon's Theory of Leadership (see Introduction, p. 3). Unlike the so-called Classical virtues of wisdom (*sophia*), justice (*dikaiosunê*), self-restraint (*sôphrosunê*), and courage (*aretê*), which are often regarded as unequivocally good,[1] the love of humanity, the love of learning, and the love of being honored can in fact be as much of a liability to a leader as an asset.

In what follows, I do not mean to assert that the specific terms, *philanthrôpia*, *philomatheia*, and *philotîmia*, were always or even usually used in an ambivalent way. What I am asserting is that the underlying ideas that these terms captured were highly problematic for leaders and that Xenophon's predecessors and contemporaries were well aware of this. The terms in question were more often than not used to capture the positive, unproblematic side of these concepts. It is this positive side, and the extent to which Xenophon's Cyrus avoids the negative sides, that I am trying to understand in this chapter and the following two. I will attempt to contextualize each of the problems I identify with examples from Xenophon and his contemporaries. In some cases, for the purpose of clarity, I will use examples that come after Xenophon or that otherwise likely had no

---

[1] There are some rare exceptions to this rule. Xenophon's Socrates points out that a reputation for wisdom might lead to enslavement at the hands of a king who wished to utilize the person's wisdom (*Memorabilia* 4.2.33). Euripides' Phaedra engages in a verbal war with Hippolytus over the proper meaning of self-restraint. In her death, she vows to teach Hippolytus (who is devoted to chastity) to restrain his self-restraint (*Hippolytus* 667, 730–731, 1034–1035). The interlocutors in Plato's *Republic* entertain the idea that justice might be a disadvantage for those who practice it (cf. Thrasymachus' remarks at 343d–344c), only to conclude that, along with the other three "Classical" virtues, it is one of the greatest goods.

direct influence on him. They nonetheless depict circumstances similar to what we see Cyrus facing in his leadership and they help to illustrate the pervasiveness of these problems in the ancient (and modern) world. Additionally, given their extent, these problems may be studied in greater detail in future work on ancient leadership.

Thus far into our study, we have seen places where it would be inaccurate to say that Xenophon pursues an absolutist notion of what it means to be a good leader, but rather a more relativistic or situational one. For example, the boy Cyrus evinces a situational view of beauty when he declares both his father, the king of the Persians, and his grandfather, the king of the Medes to be "most beautiful" (*kallistos*). The former is the perfect example of the modest style of Persian dress and the latter excels more luxuriously "in processions and at the Medan court" (1.3.2). We saw in Chapter One (pp. 28–29, 33) that Cyrus is good at forging relationships between others ("match-making"), but that he also tries to weaken the bonds even among family members in order to diminish the likelihood that anyone might plot against him. It is thus not always necessary for a leader to "bring people together" or to "divide them," but to perform each of these tasks to the extent that it preserves the security and reputation of the leader as well as the prosperity of the followers—a delicate balancing act, to be sure.

Cyrus also seems to take a morally relativistic stance on the emotion of envy. He tells Tigranes to forgive his father for executing his tutor (3.1.40) and he weeps for his uncle when Cyaxares admits to envying the affection Cyrus receives from the Medes (5.5.35). Nevertheless, Cyrus pursues the Assyrian king with a vengeance for his actions committed out of envy against Gadatas and the son of Gobryas (4.6.2.9, 5.2.7–8, 5.3.19). Though morally similar, these acts have vastly different political significance and, accordingly, Cyrus as a leader forgives the envy in the former cases but not in the latter.

Xenophon expands on the relativistic nature of leadership in a passage in the *Memorabilia* where he has Socrates explain generalship to a young man intent on becoming a general:

> καὶ γὰρ παρασκευαστικὸν τῶν εἰς τὸν πόλεμον τὸν στρατηγὸν εἶναι χρή, καὶ ποριστικὸν τῶν ἐπιτηδείων τοῖς στρατιώταις, καὶ μηχανικὸν καὶ ἐργαστικὸν καὶ ἐπιμελῆ καὶ καρτερικὸν καὶ ἀγχίνουν, καὶ <u>φιλόφρονά τε καὶ ὠμόν, καὶ ἁπλοῦν τε καὶ ἐπίβουλον, καὶ φυλακτικόν τε καὶ κλέπτην, καὶ προετικὸν καὶ ἅρπαγα καὶ φιλόδωρον καὶ πλεονέκτην καὶ ἀσφαλῆ καὶ ἐπιθετικόν</u>, καὶ ἄλλα πολλὰ καὶ φύσει καὶ ἐπιστήμῃ δεῖ τὸν εὖ στρατηγήσοντα ἔχειν.

It is necessary for the general to be a provider of the equipment of war and a supplier of the soldiers' necessities. And he must be resourceful, energetic, attentive, hardy, and shrewd. *He must be both friendly and harsh, both sincere and crafty, both a protector and a thief, both lavish and rapacious, generous and greedy, cautious and ready to attack.* And it is necessary for the man intending to be a good general to possess many other qualities either through nature or knowledge.[2]

Memorabilia 3.1.6

In examining the fourteen problems before us, we will see how well Cyrus balances the contradictory roles of leadership. We begin with six problems associated with *philanthrôpia*.

Getting Close but Not Too Close

Cyrus' *philanthrôpia* involves a fondness for the company of others, benefaction, and expressions of sympathy and encouragement. But how well does Cyrus resist the ways in which these feelings may be manipulated? A fable has come down to us from Aesop in which a farmer happens upon a frozen viper (*Fabulae* 62). As a gesture of *philanthrôpia*, he places the viper inside his shirt to warm it, only to be bitten and killed when the viper thaws. The moral of the story, says Aesop, is that one should not show pity to the irredeemably wicked. The Spartan Clearchus, though not known for his fondness for others, makes a similar mistake by allowing himself to be charmed by the friendly gestures (*philophrosunê*) of the treacherous satrap Tissaphernes (*Anabasis* 2.5.27–34). We have also seen how Astyages in Ctesias' *Persica* shows kindness to Cyrus, only to lament that he has been betrayed by him in the end (p. 26). During the Peloponnesian War the Athenians debate whether to spare or put to death the Mytilenians who have revolted from the Delian League. The statesman Cleon argues famously that they must not spare the Mytilenians because "*pity, pleasure in speeches, and indulgence*" are most detrimental to their empire (Thucydides *Histories* 3.40.2). To grant them this indulgence, he says, would invite further rebellion because no city would fear Athenian reprisal. In perhaps the most famous example from ancient literature of how feelings of kindness may be manipulated, Sinon in Virgil's *Aeneid* persuades the Trojans to wheel the Trojan Horse inside their walls. He treacherously wins their trust and pity by describing the many ways that his kinsmen, the Argives, have betrayed him (2.195–198).

---

[2]   Cf. the discussion of tactics between Cyrus and his father (*Cyropaedia* 1.6.14).

Xenophon's Cyrus is more cautious than Virgil's Trojans, despite his *philan-thrôpia*. Cyrus treats his enemies with a careful blend of friendship and caution—even ruthlessness. When the Hyrcanians intimate their desire to defect to Cyrus from the Assyrian army, he offers to welcome them as friends; but if they show any signs of hostility, he instructs his men "to leave no one alive" (*Cyropaedia* 4.2.18). Cyrus forms a friendship with the Assyrian nobleman Gobryas, who had defected from the Assyrian king because the king had treacherously killed Gobryas' son. Cyrus is invited to win honor by avenging the son and to join Gobryas inside his castle. He proceeds more cautiously than Clearchus in the *Anabasis*. Rather than march directly into the castle and risk his entire army, Cyrus surveys the area and tests it for a possible ambush, a precaution Gobryas invites him to engage in:

> When all of his men were outside, Gobryas told Cyrus to enter however he thought was safest. So Cyrus sent in some scouts and his forces and, accordingly, went in himself. When he had entered, keeping the gates wide open, he summoned all his friends and the officers of those with him.
>
> *Cyropaedia* 5.2.6

Cyrus checks his natural impulse to treat Gobryas as a friend by being attentive to his own self-interest and the well-being of his army. Furthermore, Cyrus turns down Gobryas' offers of abundant wealth—and his daughter—showing not only that he practices *philanthrôpia* with restraint but that he practices restraint against the temptations of royal sovereignty, grand fortresses, and even women "worthy of erotic love" (cf. ἀξιέραστα, 5.2.9.9).

In fact, whereas romance abounds in the *Cyropaedia* (e.g. between Tigranes and his wife, Croesus and his wife, and especially Pantheia and Abradatas), Cyrus does not take a wife until the very end of his adventures. For Tatum, Cyrus' detachment from others has seemed problematic:

> Although the broad divisions of family, friends, and enemies are real enough, we shall find it hard to see any difference in Cyrus' treatment of his family, friends, or enemies. At every stage of his career, and at every level of involvement with others, he has *a curious detachment about other people*, even as he makes himself famous throughout the world for his kindness and his generosity, through calculated shows of philanthropy.
>
> Tatum 71 (my italics)

For all his affection for others, Cyrus does not allow love to compromise with his goals as a leader. Yet Xenophon seems to endorse this position, as we have seen (p. 70), when he has Ischomachus explain that romantic love is one of the greatest obstacles to a person learning to be attentive (*Oeconomicus* 12.5). And ancient literature abounds with accounts of leaders who were, or appeared to be, tragically distracted by love for another: Paris, Agamemnon, Mark Antony, Aeneas.

Nor do preexisting friendships cloud Cyrus' judgment or distract him from his ambitions. When Cyrus subdues the Armenians (they owed tribute to the Medes and were planning to revolt), he must decide whether to put them to death, which the Armenian king himself admits would be just. This occasion is ripe for the pity that Cyrus shows elsewhere: the king's son, Tigranes, is a childhood friend and hunting-companion of Cyrus; he is newly married; he appears suddenly to plead for his family and weeps at the sight of their captivity (3.1.7). Cyrus gazes upon Tigranes in this condition but withholds any gesture of friendliness toward him (cf. οὐδὲν ἐφιλοφρονήσατο αὐτῷ, 3.1.8.2). This scene might have aroused Cyrus' pity, but Xenophon highlights Cyrus' self-restraint, a trait central to the Persian educational system (1.2.6–8). After showing restraint, Cyrus invites everyone to attend the trial of the king, including the women, and then allows Tigranes to plead his father's case. Consistent with Cyrus' lack of friendly gesture, Tigranes makes no appeals to pity (or justice), but rather argues that it is in Cyrus' self-interest to spare the royal family (3.1.14). Their friendship is renewed only after Cyrus has established that he can again trust Tigranes and his father. In other words, Cyrus makes sure that the "viper" is in fact not irredeemably wicked, a task that requires him to be an extraordinary judge of character, both his own and that of others.

Being Friendly but Not Permissive

Sometimes it is difficult for the "philanthropic" leader to take an interest in discipline. In his eulogy to the Boeotian general Proxenus in the *Anabasis*, Xenophon captures well how leadership may suffer when a leader tries too hard to be a "nice guy":

> He [Proxenus] was capable of leading gentlemen, yet he could not fashion any fear or reverence for himself in the soldiers, but he was more diffident toward them than his subordinates were toward himself. And he was more afraid to appear to be disliked by his soldiers than his soldiers were of disobeying him. And he believed that in order

to be and to seem to be a general it was enough to praise those who
behaved properly and to withhold praise from those who misbehaved.
As a result the gentlemen in his company were kindly disposed toward
him, but the unjust plotted against him as someone easy to manipulate.

Anabasis 2.6.19–20

The Roman general and triumvir, Mark Antony, had no trouble being friends
with his soldiers and he had a legacy of *philanthrôpia* that he inherited from
his father (Plutarch *Life of Antony* 1.2–3, 4.4). Like Cyrus, he was merciful to the
conquered, fond of hosting banquets, and even a helpful facilitator of his friends'
love affairs. Yet Plutarch says Antony was reluctant to hear complaints or issue
judgments. He was moreover prone to manipulation by flatterers. As a result he
was an embarrassment to his friend, Julius Caesar, and lost the respect of the
leading men in Rome (6.5–6, 24.6–8). This kind of permissiveness is not only bad
for the leader, however. Alexander the Great is said to have been so generous
that his followers grew luxurious and slothful (Plutarch *Life of Alexander* 40, 41).
The tendency for "soft countries to breed soft men" is of course thematic of
Herodotus' *Histories*, with the Persians being the prime example, and we see the
same effects of spoils on Cyaxares and other Medes in the *Cyropaedia* (4.1.13–14,
4.2.11).

Cyrus, however, does not show care for others in such a way as to let
them become decadent; nor does he lose their respect. He is equally severe in
punishing wrongdoers and careful to ensure that his followers do not become
lax through his generosity.[3] If prisoners of war try to escape, they are killed
and their spoils go to their captors (4.5.6). If Cyrus' soldiers sack and plunder a
city (e.g. Sardis) without regard to fairness or safety, he upbraids them for their
disobedience and ensures that only the obedient receive a prize (7.2.4–8). Such
discipline is consistent with the education he receives from Cambyses (1.6.20).
When Cyrus sets up a palace in Babylon, he challenges his followers to maintain
their empire with strict attention to virtue and compels them pay court to him
by taking away the property of those who fail to do so (7.5.85, 8.1.20). The fear
that Cyrus inspires in such instances complements his ability to win enthusiastic gratitude through his numerous forms of *philanthrôpia*. Both gratitude and
fear, Xenophon says, were the feelings that bound his vast empire (cf. τῷ ἀφ'
ἑαυτοῦ φόβῳ ... ἐπιθυμίαν ... τοῦ αὐτῷ χαρίζεσθαι, 1.1.5).

---

[3]   Cyrus the Younger is also known for harsh punishments, despite his good will (*Anabasis* 1.9.13).

Loving Everyone to the Proper Degree

In Greek literature, gods regularly have their favorites, for whom they feel fondness, admiration, or concern; but when the gods feel *philanthrôpia*, they seem to feel it indiscriminately. Prometheus gives fire to *mortals*—not to mortals of a certain type, to mortals who follow a special rite of worship, or to mortals who "deserve" it. The same is true for the "philanthropic" Eros, as Plato presents him in the *Symposium*, or Cronus in the *Laws*. Xenophon's Socrates asserts that the gods manifest their *philanthrôpia* by providing humanity with everything from the sun and the earth to food and the capacity for reason.[4]

As we have already seen, Xenophon and Isocrates see divine and mortal *philanthrôpia* as somewhat analogous, at least in powerful leaders (Chapter One, pp. 42–43). We might say that wanting to benefit one's followers is a leader's primary motive or goal and thus that *philanthrôpia* is crucial. Few people would follow a leader who did not take into account their wellbeing at least part of the time. Agamemnon seems to assume that his good will toward his men is crucial for their allegiance, for he tells the Achaeans at Troy that he will give back Chryseis to her father in order to stop Apollo's plague because he wants the army "to be safe rather than perish" (*Iliad* 1.116). Similarly, Socrates argues to Thrasymachus that "all forms of rule, in so far as it is rule, look out for what is best for no one other than that person who is being ruled and tended to, both in civic and private rule" (*Republic* 345d). Xenophon's Socrates says of Agamemnon that "a king is chosen not so that he may take beneficial thought for himself, but so that he may benefit those who chose him" (*Memorabilia* 3.2.2; cf. *Agesilaus* 7.1). Yet leaders, unlike gods, are not immortal and they do not have a fixed or permanent sovereignty. Thus, despite the connotations of the term, *philanthrôpia* for mortals is not, in practice, indiscriminate. This is to say that *philanthrôpia* cannot involve loving all of humanity, all of the time, in the same ways, and to the same degree. Leaders must regularly balance the more immediate interests, claims, and merits of family, friends, lovers, and fellow-citizens against those of another city-state, another country, or even strangers who have virtually no affiliation with anyone.[5]

This dilemma is at the forefront of the dramatic conflict for many kings in Greek Tragedy. In several plots (what Burian has called "Suppliant Plays") the king of a city-state is asked to receive refugees that are being pursued by

---

[4]   Plato *Laws* 713d6; *Memorabilia* 4.3.5.6, 4.3.7.7. Cf. Martin 1961:174, Nikolaidis 1980:352n17 on *philanthrôpia* as a civilizing impulse.

[5]   That this is a universal challenge may be readily observed in the case of the average American senator who may be expected to care about her constituents, her country, her donors, her friends, her family, and even those who are not citizens of the United States. For *philanthrôpia* as a concern for those outside a familiar community cf. Azoulay 2004b:319–326.

someone from another city-state who threatens to reclaim them by force.[6] The question for the king then becomes should he care more for the suppliants or for his own city, which will come under attack for harboring fugitives? Theseus, the king of Athens in Sophocles' *Oedipus at Colonus*, is one such example. He must decide whether to receive Oedipus and his daughter, Antigone, as suppliants into his city, risking a war with Creon, king of Thebes, who has learned from an oracle that Oedipus' body may be used to ensure victory in war. Often there is encouragement from the gods to receive the suppliant; or the suppliant may have familial ties to the petitioned king. Oedipus, however, has no familial tie to Theseus or to Athens; moreover, he is blind, aged, and rather disagreeable. So, there are many reasons not to want to help him. Nevertheless, Theseus risks his city's safety to help Oedipus out of what we might call *philanthrôpia* (though Sophocles does not use this term). He is motivated partly by piety and partly because Oedipus' tomb will be a blessing to Athens. Perhaps most importantly, however, Theseus acts because, as a fellow human being, he knows what it is like to suffer the misfortunes of an exile (551–568).[7] Other kings in these "Suppliant Plays" face this same dilemma.[8]

This problematic aspect of *philanthrôpia* can be so acute as to make us wonder whether powerful leaders can have close friends or lovers at all.[9] In general, any kindness done to a friend or family member is potentially one *not done* to a citizen or a stranger, and may thus arouse envy or resentment. Or, in the case of Theseus above, any kindness done to a stranger may put at risk those more intimately connected to the leader. How much relative weight then should the leader assign to the roles of a *philos*, *philetairos*, *philopolis*, *philellên*, or *philanthrôpos*? Perhaps no other Greek leader had to face this question as much as Alexander the Great (at least as he is described by Plutarch), whose character and career greatly resemble Cyrus'. Despite his benevolence, generosity, and thoughtfulness, Alexander had to weigh the interests of his mother Olympias, his fellow Macedonian nobles and countrymen, the citizens of a conquered Greece, the members of the Persian Empire that he would eventually conquer, his own intimate band of comrades, as well as his lover and best friend Hephestion (Plutarch *Life of Alexander* 39.1–3). In one instance, Alexander tries

---

[6]   See Burian 1974 on the generic features of a "Suppliant Play."

[7]   Cf. Sandridge 436–440.

[8]   Cf. Pelasgus (Aeschylus *Suppliants* 474–89), Aegeus (Euripides *Medea* 689–745), Demophon (Euripides *Children of Heracles* 236–46), as well as a Euripidean Theseus (Euripides *Suppliants* 334–45).

[9]   It is debatable how important it was for kings in the ancient world to enjoy true friendship (*philia*), whereby we mean such notions as regarding the friend as a "second self" and revealing one's entire self to the friend. Konstan 1997b argues that friendship was not celebrated as a "royal virtue" until Dio Chrysostom's *Third Kingship Oration* (c. 100 CE).

to strike a balance and to end a rivalry between two close friends by dubbing Hephestion "friend of Alexander" (*philalexandros*) and Craterus the "friend of the king" (*philobasilês*) (*Life of Alexander* 47.5–7).

Cyrus confronts this question of balance throughout the *Cyropaedia*. He must manage his ties to family (especially Cyaxares), friends (both upper-class Medan and Persian), fellow-citizens, and the members of the many other nations that he conquers and incorporates (Armenians, Chaldaeans, Hyrcanians, Sacians, Assyrians, Egyptians). As a rule, Cyrus seems to eschew any more personal ties and loyalties over considerations of fairness and also self-interest. We noted above that Cyrus has no time for love until the end of his campaigns. Moreover, the relationship he forms with his wife, the daughter of Cyaxares, though affectionate, is largely political (it unites the Persian and Medan nations). In other instances of justice and politics over personal preference, Cyrus invites the "uneducated" Persian commoners to join the Persian army and thereby gives them an opportunity to distinguish themselves according to their virtue (2.2.21). He incorporates numerous kings and peoples from other nations into his empire and awards them places of prominence. We have also seen where he expands the language of family to include even non-Persians (Chapter One, p. 41).

Cyrus does not submit to feelings of sympathy even among his closest friends, especially when it would be unfair to do so. In Book Eight, his devoted Persian comrade Hystaspas approaches him at a banquet to ask why Cyrus has shown greater honor to Chrysantas (8.4.9–12). Again, as in the Tigranes episode, this appeal might have elicited Cyrus' pity or special fondness for a friend who sees himself as overlooked by his commanding officer. Instead, Cyrus registers no sympathy but gives Hystaspas a precise explanation for his preference for Chrysantas: Chrysantas is not only the more obedient follower but he also modifies Cyrus' commands in order to accomplish what is best for Cyrus and everyone else. Hystaspas, for his part, wants to be rewarded for his true virtues and thus accepts Cyrus' explanation, apparently inspired by the guidance it provides him. Perhaps to soften the blow, Cyrus soon arranges for a marriage between Hystaspas and the daughter of Gobryas, again on the basis of Hystaspas' worthiness (8.4.26). By managing even his closest friendships according to merit, Cyrus discourages his friends from rivaling one another on the extraneous grounds of personal fondness, childhood or familial ties, or shared personal interests. Additionally, Cyrus ensures that his comrades continue to rival one another in obedience and thoughtfulness, lest they ever band together against their leader (8.2.28).

Yet, this principle of justice is applied by Xenophon's Cyrus only so far. At the end of the narrative, the empire he governs still privileges the Persians, and the highest honor in the land, kingship itself, is a hereditary one. Much as Cyrus' fondness for competitions moves the empire in the direction of a pure meritocracy, he does not achieve one. Had Xenophon tried to portray a meritocracy, he might have portrayed Cyrus engaged in some kind of selection process through the Persian educational system he brings to Babylon. But there is no indication that his son, Cambyses, had to succeed in any trial to inherit his father's kingdom. On his deathbed, Cyrus appoints Cambyses to the throne over his younger son on three grounds: that he has more experience (being older), that Persians believe in respecting their elders on all fronts, and that the succession of the eldest son is both the legal and the time-tested procedure (8.7.9–11). Moreover, Cyrus claims that forming ties on the basis of blood relation is most preferable (8.7.14–15).

After Cyrus dies, Xenophon is quick to point out the destructive rivalry that emerges between his sons and the precipitous decline of the Persian Empire. There are of course two ways to interpret this decline: Cyrus is such a great leader that the Persians are nothing without him; or Cyrus is a good leader but ultimately flawed for not establishing a succession of leaders, or a system of government, as virtuous as himself. Plato blames Cyrus specifically for not overseeing his children's education, allowing them instead to be raised by women and eunuchs in the Medan style (*Laws* 695a–b). It is certainly worth asking why Xenophon does not present a Cyrus who could leave behind a better institution.

We may give several, perhaps not entirely satisfactory answers. First is an argument from the "nature of things." Xenophon asserts at the beginning of the *Cyropaedia* that all forms of government eventually deteriorate even over a short period of time, though he does not explain why this happens of necessity. He suggests that humans simply cannot lead other humans as well as animals. At the end of Book One, he has Cambyses explain that many states have fallen because of ill-advised attacks against others and the mistreatment of their friends (1.6.45). Second, Xenophon suggests that a government, regardless of the quality of its laws, is only as good as the character of its leaders. "Whenever the person in charge is better," he says, "the laws are implemented more purely; but whenever the person is worse, their implementation is sloppy" (8.1.8). A few pages later, Xenophon says that Cyrus regards the good ruler as a "seeing law," who not only gives instructions but also observes and punishes the one who fails to carry them out (8.1.22). In the absence of Cyrus, then, it seems no institution is invulnerable. Third, Xenophon gives little reason to assume that a son will have the same character as his ancestors. Even though Cyrus agrees with his father, Cambyses, on the precepts of leadership, he still requires training from him to develop into the leader that he becomes (there is no indication that Cyrus educates his own son, Cambyses). Yet Cyrus does not resemble Astyages much at all, nor does Tigranes particularly resemble his father, nor the Assyrian king his father.[10]

Fourth, Xenophon was somewhat bound by Persian history, at least as the Greeks understood it. Cambyses (the son of Cyrus) was seen as a degenerate king in several sources; Herodotus depicts him committing varied forms of hubris against family, friends, and enemies. And, however great it may have been in the past,[11] Persian culture was seen to be on the decline; Xenophon was thus left to account for these "facts" in his portrait of Cyrus. The best that he could come up with, it seems, was to portray a father holding fast to the custom (even if an unfair one) of primogeniture and trying desperately to stave off the degeneration that Xenophon and his readers were likely to see in the aftermath of his reign. If Cyrus had been an "ideal" leader, he might have applied justice to his "philanthropic" impulse consistently, even with his own sons. That depiction, however, would have flown in the face of perceived history. We should note that in making this criticism of Cyrus we are going beyond the bounds of Xenophon's treatment of him; Xenophon gives no indication that Cyrus is somehow to blame for not ensuring the continued success of the Persian Empire. The most we may infer from what he does say is that Cyrus could not ensure the prosperity of Persia because human beings are very hard to lead and neither of the sons of Cyrus had his extraordinary character.

Proper Rivalries

By being open to so many friends, the "philanthropic" leader may also be open to many enemies. In his generosity he may threaten the reputation of others or elevate his closest comrades to his own level. Alexander is portrayed as "prone to lavish giving" (*megalodôrotatos*) in a "spirit of good will" (*philophrosunê*), so much so that his mother, Olympias, cautions him against making all his friends "co-kings" while bankrupting himself (Plutarch *Life of Alexander* 39.1–5).[12] Cyrus arouses a similar concern in the Lydian king, Croesus, who believes that Cyrus may have given away all of his resources and compromised his own safety (*Cyropaedia* 8.2.13–23).

Philanthrôpia is a public act and to that extent it can be subjected to criticism and rivalry. One aspiring benefactor may not be able to benefit the people as much as another. Or, he might himself become a beneficiary and reduced to

---

[10] The elder Assyrian king feels pity and sympathy for Gobryas when the Assyrian prince kills his son, but not so the prince himself. The elder king is virtuous whereas the son is wicked (4.6.5).

[11] Miller 1997 is a valuable source for Athenian perspectives on Persia and its apparent decline.

[12] Note the rivalry between Alexander and Philotas, the son of Parmenio (Plutarch *Life of Alexander* 48).

a humbler station. Ferguson has noted an implicit condescension in many acts of *philanthrôpia*, and Gera formulates this rivalry in zero-sum terms: "for every happy benefactor there must be a humiliated recipient."[13] Prometheus is the first and most obvious example. As Hephaestus chains him to the Scythian cliffs, he pronounces his sentence: "Such things have you reaped for yourself from your 'philanthropic' tendency; for, though a god, you did not tremble before the anger of the gods and granted honors to mortals beyond what is right."[14] In rescuing the goddess Peace from beneath a mound of stones, the "most philanthropic" Hermes also transgresses a mandate from Zeus (Aristophanes *Peace* 371–372). The physician Asclepius brings a man back from the dead and is struck down by Zeus' lightning (Pindar *Pythian Odes* 3.54–60). Socrates earns a bad reputation for generously sharing his wisdom with anyone he can. The Athenians prosecute him because his *philanthrôpia* corrupts the youth and ultimately undermines the authority of the city. Socrates, too, is severely punished.[15]

For his part, Cyrus rivals his uncle and the king of the Medes, Cyaxares. This rivalry has several sources beyond Cyrus' *philanthrôpia* and builds over time. The boy Cyrus succeeds at hunting, for which Cyaxares dubs him already a "king" (1.4.9). When Cyrus pursues some Assyrians in a skirmish, Cyaxares joins the chase out of shame (1.4.22). On campaign against the Assyrians, Cyrus regularly contradicts Cyaxares' orders and proposals (2.4.5, 3.3.31, 3.3.47, 3.3.56). Cyaxares envies Cyrus' eagerness to wage war on the Assyrians but is too timid, as well as too drawn to luxury, to campaign with him (4.1.13). As this rivalry comes to a head, Cyaxares rationalizes his anger toward Cyrus, complaining that Cyrus had left him in a vulnerable position while pursuing personal glory. The more accurate explanation, however, seems to be that Cyrus has outdone Cyaxares in showing *philanthrôpia*. By doing so many good deeds for the Medes, he has stolen their affection from Cyaxeres, as one might steal the affection of someone's most beloved companion. Cyaxares says:

> What if someone were to show so much attention to your wife so as to make her love him more than yourself, would you then delight in this

---

[13] Ferguson 1958:105–106, Gera 1993:106.

[14] Cf. φιλανθρώπου ... τρόπου, *Prometheus Bound* 28–30. Prometheus' friendly feeling toward mortals and the wrath of the gods that it elicits is referenced twice more (119–123, 239–241).

[15] *Euthyphro* 3d7. Ferguson 1958:105–106, incorrectly I believe, sees Socrates' *philanthrôpia* in this passage as containing an element of condescension on Socrates' part, rather than a condescension perceived by the Athenians. The term seems to be used to make the point that Euthyphro has a form of wisdom that cannot be transferred (and thus is less threatening), whereas Socrates, as a generous "philanthropist," can contaminate the whole city with his wisdom.

benefaction? Far from it, I think. But I think that in treating you this way he would be doing the greatest injustice of all.

Cyropaedia 5.5.30

Even if Cyaxares seems ungrateful, envious, and petty here, his perspective is morally defensible according to one of Cyrus' own prior judgments. When Cyrus attempts to reconcile Tigranes with his father, the Armenian king, over the execution of Tigranes' tutor, the king explains that he had killed the tutor out of envy, in the spirit of a man who discovers that his wife has been seduced by an adulterer. Cyrus instructs Tigranes to forgive his father because he did not act out of malice toward him; it was, he says, a "human mistake" (3.1.39–40). Moreover, as we have seen, Cyrus himself uses *philanthrôpia* (in the form of specialized gift-giving) to prevent his followers from forming intimate attachments with one another that could divide their loyalty to him.

So the problem remains: how can an ambitious leader in a subordinate role (such as Cyrus) manage to excel in *philanthrôpia* without offending an officially superior (but actually inferior) leader? We might expect the rivalry to become public and irreversible, with the subordinate leader simply challenging and eventually supplanting his rival. So great was Alexander's rivalry with his father, Philip, that he may have plotted his assassination (Plutarch *Life of Alexander* 5.2, 10.4). Cyrus the Younger, an otherwise generous and benevolent figure, plots rebellion against his older brother, Artaxerxes II.[16]

But this is not how our Cyrus handles his situation. Rather than aggravate his rivalry with Cyaxares, he manages his uncle's envy with a delicate balance of assertiveness and devotion.[17] He cautions Cyaxares not to make light of the services that he and others have performed for him. He enumerates all the ways he has benefitted Cyaxares and how these acts were designed to benefit him and were not simply a consequence of Cyrus' own ambitions. In effect, he argues that he deserves to be the dominant *philanthrôpos*. Yet, Cyrus also shows sympathy, even tears, for Cyaxares' grief. Perhaps most importantly, he remains in the subordinate role and stresses Cyaxares' authority, asking him, as his uncle, to do Cyrus the favor of forgiving him for hurting his feelings (5.5.35). Cyrus concludes this appeal by asking to give Cyaxares a kiss of deference, which Cyaxares grants. This gesture serves to allay the concerns of the Medes and Persians who watch anxiously as the two leaders work out their differences. In the end, it is a happy

---

[16] On Xenophon's attempt to downplay the treacherousness of this rebellion in the *Anabasis*, see Due 1989:191–192.

[17] Danzig 2009:292–293 calls this episode "the crowning example of the redistribution of offices during peacetime by means of persuasion and threat." He notes that Cyrus succeeds both in satisfying his own self-interest while justly avoiding violence and harm to Cyaxares.

consequence for Xenophon's narrative that Cyaxares dies lacking a male heir and can bequeath the Medan throne to Cyrus without rivalry.[18]

Cyrus' gratitude, devotion, and deference consistently offset the rivalry and implicit condescension associated with *philanthrôpia*, which, as we have already noted, can put the practitioner in the superior position of the "father."[19] We have seen in his first act of *philanthrôpia* that he has a way of insinuating himself into the families of his friends by showing affection for the sons of the Medan noblemen (1.4.1). When the Assyrian nobleman Gobryas appeals to Cyrus as a suppliant to become his son by avenging the murder of Gobryas' own child, Cyrus agrees (cf. παῖδα, 4.6.2.9; 5.2.7–8). Again, when Cyrus meets the Assyrian eunuch Gadatas, he vows that even though Gadatas cannot have children, Cyrus and his comrades will stand by him as if they were his biological children (cf. παῖδας ἐκγόνους, 5.3.19). For his part, Gadatas proclaims that he could not have asked for a better son (5.4.12). Finally, Pantheia declares that Cyrus treated Abradatas (her husband) as a brother by showing respect to his captive wife (cf. ἀδελφοῦ, 6.4.7.5). As such, Cyrus benefits others not only as a "father," but as a peer and a subordinate, even in situations where he is clearly the figure with greater authority. In this way he minimizes the implicit condescension and potential for rivalry that face the other "philanthropic" characters we have considered.

For a long time many scholars have been troubled by the level of manipulation in Cyrus' "philanthropic" ability to play up to others and anticipate their feelings.[20] Cyaxares has received special sympathy from commentators dating back to Machiavelli, who saw Cyrus' deception of Cyaxares as an unfortunate prerequisite to empire (*Discourses* 2.13.1). More recently, Rasmussen has sympathized with Cyaxares, calling him "disgraced and emasculated" and "reduced to little more than a pampered houseguest."[21] Stripped of its evaluative language Rasmussen's portrayal of Cyaxares' situation is more or less true: Cyrus does deceive him more than once, and Cyaxares does become marginalized in so many ways well before Cyrus undertakes the bulk of his campaign against the Assyrians. What Rasmussen's portrayal leaves out, and what makes the evaluative language so inappropriate, is the literary and historical context that Xenophon inherited. In all other versions of Cyrus' rise to power, Cyrus becomes king of the Medes by

---

[18] Neither Herodotus (*Histories* 1.107–130) nor Isocrates (*Evagoras* 38) portrays a harmonious rise to power for Cyrus.

[19] Cf. the exceptional gratitude in Cyrus the Younger (αἰδημονέστατος, *Anabasis* 1.9.5.2).

[20] Tatum 1989:201–204 notes Cyrus' extension of familial terms to those outside his natural family, but sees it as a primarily self-interested and manipulative move: "Cyrus plays the role of a son without really being a son at all."

[21] Rasmussen 2009:xvii.

force and by design. He feels that they do not deserve to rule over the Persians and thus conquers them in battle, relying on much more deception, betrayal, and cruelty than Xenophon's Cyrus. Nowhere does Xenophon portray Cyrus as intending to become king of the Medes. Instead he portrays Cyrus as seeking the highest honors in whatever venue he can; empire, in Xenophon's conception, is for Cyrus more or less an accident of circumstance (unless pursuing the highest honors is always tantamount to pursuing an empire).

Yet, Xenophon does not sidestep a central problem of leadership, namely, what an aspiring leader should do when subordinate to a less competent one. In an ideal picture, Cyaxares would recognize and admit his inferiority to Cyrus and simply allow him to take over. But Xenophon seems to believe that this is not how the real world works, that even the less competent need to feel important (in fact they may not even be aware of their incompetence). Thus Xenophon portrays Cyrus as "manipulating" Cyaxares in such a way as to avoid open hostility but still achieve his ambitions and what is ultimately beneficial for all parties—even for Cyaxares. By the end of the work, he is still in the magnanimous position to bequeath his daughter and his empire to Cyrus.

What Xenophon does seem to sidestep, however, is what we might think of as the ultimate rivalry between Cyrus and Cyaxares, the question of whose "house" will stand atop the Medan Empire. As Xenophon narrates it, Cyaxares has no male heirs and thus may bequeath his empire and his daughter to Cyrus without offending his (hypothetical) son. It is not clear at all how Cyrus could have remained "most philanthropic" and taken over the Medan throne from a legitimate male heir if Cyaxares had wanted to appoint his son and the son desired the position.

Giving without Losing

We have seen that Cyrus' *philanthrôpia* entails giving abundantly (*poludôria*) and sharing spoils with his men. On at least one occasion he gives on the basis of need, with no apparent consideration for his own advantage (7.1.1.4). Elsewhere, the Lydian king Croesus voices concern that Cyrus may be so recklessly generous as to compromise his own safety and advantage. Yet, Cyrus shows that his generosity has been carefully calculated to win loyal friends. As proof, he asks them to supply him with all the wealth and resources they can, which results in even more generosity than he had initially shown (8.2.15–19). Moreover, Xenophon frequently shows Cyrus as giving gifts not indiscriminately, but according to considerations of merit and, perhaps most importantly, obedience. Even as a boy, Cyrus doles out meat from his grandfather's table according to the services that each of his attendants has performed (1.3.7). Once Cyrus is in command of an army, he proposes to the infantry, and by implication to the officers, that they divide their spoils according to how each man has performed in battle (2.3.4). Cyrus himself sometimes participates in the distribution and even allows his men to appeal for greater spoils (7.5.35).[22]

Caring without Anxiety

In addition to being a political burden, caring for others can be a psychological one. In Sophocles' *Oedipus Tyrannus*, Oedipus describes this burden in order to reassure the plague-ridden citizens of Thebes that he is taking care of them. He plays up the leader-as-physician metaphor and emphasizes his "wakefulness":

> O pitiable children, you have come desiring things known and not unknown to me, for I fully understand that all of you are sick. Yet though sick, there is not one of you who is as sick as I am. *For your pain comes upon each person individually by himself and not another, whereas my soul groans for the city and myself and you equally*, to such an extent that you are not rousing me from a sound sleep, but know that I have in fact shed many a tear and have traversed many a path in the wanderings of my mind.
>
> *Oedipus the King* 58–67

For Jason in his quest for the Golden Fleece the burden of caring for his followers reaches the point of helplessness. In an assembly of his Argonauts, he says to his comrade Tiphys:

> I have been on guard every day through the grievous night, pondering all the details, ever since you first assembled for my sake. You converse at your ease because you are concerned about your own life. Yet, while I am troubled not in the least for my own lot, I am fearful for this man and that man and equally for you and my other comrades, if I do not bring you back safely to the land of Hellas.[23]
>
> Apollonius *Argonautica* 2.631–637, translation Race

For all of its benefits, material and psychological, striving to help others takes its toll on Cyrus. As we have seen, young Cyrus' father tells him that as

---

[22]   The leader's challenge of dividing up spoils fairly is of course at the very foundation of the conflict of Homer's *Iliad* 1, when Agamemnon deprives Achilles of the prize of Briseis after she had been awarded to him by merit.

[23]   Scholars have doubted the sincerity of Jason's speech here (the narrator even says that Jason is "testing" his comrades at Apollonius *Argonautica* 2.638). Nevertheless, Jason's sentiment wins the sympathy and enthusiastic support of his comrades.

a leader he will have to do more than everyone else, which will include losing sleep, while he devises ways to take care of his army:

> You must keep it well in mind that all those you expect to obey you will themselves expect you to make plans on their behalf. So never be careless, but during the night plan out what your followers will do for you when the day comes, and during the day take thought for how things will go best at night.

> *Cyropaedia* 1.6.42

Cyrus observes that whereas the Medes surpass others in luxury and sleep, a leader must not win fame for easy living but for forethought and the love of toil (1.6.8). How does Cyrus manage the stress of these responsibilities?

For most of his life, as Xenophon describes it, Cyrus seems immune to anxiety. Yet, at the end of his adventures, after conquering the Assyrians in Babylon, Cyrus establishes himself as a king and assumes new and stressful responsibilities (7.5.37). One of his first initiatives is to hear the appeals of all citizens, one by one, so that he may know as much about the affairs of his kingdom as possible.[24] This plan quickly backfires: Cyrus complains that he is given no time to help his most trusted friends, no leisure time, and no time to be alone (7.5.42–45). He is, as it were, on the verge of becoming like the Persian commoner Pheraulas, overburdened with the management of his vast empire (see Chapter One, p. 37). He confesses to his comrades that he must find a way to reconcile his own interests with the interests of those he must care for.[25]

Cyrus first solicits advice from his friends on how to solve this problem, a move which itself begins to relieve him by dividing the mental burden of devising new ideas. Additionally, he devises for himself several prudent remedies to rule his kingdom in ways that remove the psychological burden and keep him safe from what he now acknowledges to be a most bellicose city (7.5.58). He adopts Chrysantas' proposal to establish a royal palace for himself (7.5.57). He surrounds himself with faithful and brave eunuchs (7.5.61). He appoints numerous overseers to the different functions of government, including tax collectors and superintendents of horses and hounds (8.1.9). As we saw in the discussion of his *philokalia* (love of beauty), he applies the extensive system of military organization (*eutaxis*) to the government, whereby he, as king, is responsible only for a few leaders at the top, who are then responsible for

---

[24] Cf. Xenophon's accessibility in the *Anabasis* (Anderson 126–127) and that of Agesilaus (Due 1989:196).

[25] Cf. ὥστε καλῶς ἔχειν τά τε ἡμέτερα καὶ τὰ τῶν ἄλλων ὧν ἡμᾶς δεῖ ἐπιμελεῖσθαι, 7.5.47.4–5.

others, on down the chain of command. With this arrangement Xenophon notes that Cyrus was able to alleviate his anxiety:

> It came to be for Cyrus that by communicating with a few people no part of his affairs went uncared for, and from this arrangement he enjoyed more leisure than anyone else who watches over a single household or a single ship.
>
> *Cyropaedia* 8.1.14–16

Conclusion

From the preceding examples of six problems that may arise from the practice of *philanthrôpia*, we have seen that it is not a "stand-alone" virtue, but one that needs the support, or constraint, of other character traits: self-restraint, justice, prudence, severity, obedience, organization (*eutaxis*), and self-mastery. As we saw in Chapter Three, many of these qualities themselves are often the result of the more fundamental traits of *philomatheia* and *philotîmia*. We have also seen that though Xenophon's presentation of *philanthrôpia* stands up to many tests, it does not survive them all: Cyrus shows undeserved favor to his son and he wins an uncontested favor from Cyaxares (i.e. he does not have to supplant him to become king of the Medes). In the former case, Cyrus shows *philanthrôpia* without considerations of justice and, in the latter case, Cyrus is allowed to fulfill his ambitions without behaving in an "unphilanthropic" way. We will continue to test the comprehensiveness of Cyrus' *philomatheia* and *philotîmia* in the next two chapters.

5

Five Problems with Loving to Learn

*P*RIMA FACIE THE LOVE OF LEARNING should be the least problematic of any leadership trait. Obviously all leaders need to know things and pay attention to things in order to help their followers, but this is not all that a love of learning in the context of leadership entails. A love of learning can be distracting: fascinating subjects unrelated to ethics and politics might cause the leader to lose interest in the mundane affairs of state. The leader might be so learned as to become clever, manipulative, or revolutionary. Intelligence might make the leader unintelligible to the followers. Finally, all the time spent in the library and away from the gymnasium might render the leader physically weak, cowardly, or contemptuous of the "less-sophisticated" followers.

Studying what Matters

Many problems for leaders who "love to learn" are illustrated by Aristophanes' portrayal of Socrates in the *Clouds* (c. 416 B.C.E.). In the play, Socrates heads the "Thinkery" (*Phrontisterion*), an institution bearing a rough resemblance to a modern university. As the "headmaster," Socrates has been invested with most of the trappings of a fifth-century sophist, "a man, usually a foreigner, who possessed arcane knowledge and had untraditional, often counter-intuitive ideas, and who offered to teach these to anyone who could afford the high tuition fees."[1] He has been tasked by Strepsiades, an Athenian farmer, to help him use clever language to escape his creditors at court. As soon as he arrives at the Thinkery, Strepsiades learns that its members are not very interested in issues relevant to the lives of the average citizen. Instead they study trivial things like

---

[1] Henderson 1988:155. Although this description of the sophist is a conventional one, recent work by Tell and others has demonstrated that the meaning of the term is one fashioned by Plato largely to discredit many contemporaries and predecessors for whom no blanket term was apt or consistent. Tell 2011:19 notes several scholars who have argued that in the fifth century the Athenian public did not distinguish sophists from philosophers. As I discuss below, Xenophon uses the term "sophist" in both a positive and negative way. As many have noted, Tigranes' sophist in the *Cyropaedia* is very much a (philosophical) Socratic figure.

the distance a flea can hop or the nominal forms of the male and female duck.[2] The problem from a leadership perspective is that Socrates and his associates are not interested in the knowledge of leadership, namely, politics and ethics.[3] The historical Socrates himself seems to have been done in by the perception that he was interested more in astronomy, cosmology, or metaphysics.[4]

No doubt with Socrates in mind, Plato notes that even the leader's *apparent* fascination with irrelevant subjects could be a liability. In his famous ship-of-state allegory in the *Republic*, he explains that the would-be captain, who understands how astronomy may be used properly to guide the ship, will be misunderstood and criticized as a "star-gazer" by the ignorant crew (488b–e).

The study of irrelevant subjects was characteristic of actual political leaders as well. Plutarch recounts an anecdote from the life of Pericles, in which the Athenian statesman and his sophist friends spend an evening debating the exact cause of death of a man who had accidentally been hit with a javelin. They wonder whether it was the thrower of the javelin, the javelin itself, or the men who had instituted such games (*Life of Pericles* 36). Their concern is less with the fact that an innocent person has died than with an academic question of causality.

Isocrates seeks to limit Alexander's pursuit of knowledge, advising him to love wisdom "not foolishly but with sense" (cf. φιλόσοφος, οὐκ ἀφρόνως ἀλλὰ νοῦν ἐχόντως, *To Alexander* 2). He praises Alexander first for associating with people who do not have an interest in base pleasures but in philosophy (he may have Alexander's teacher, Aristotle, in mind). Alexander is also to be commended for not taking up "eristic" disputations that equip young students to argue for the sake of argument. Instead, he pursues the more proper study of rhetoric, which teaches how to instruct others, form sound judgments, and praise and blame as necessary.[5]

As we have already noted in our study of Cyrus' *philomatheia* in Chapter Two (pp. 46–49), Cyrus' love of learning is in almost every instance circumscribed by his desire to win honor (in hunting and warfare) or to help others. Achieving each of these goals entails knowledge of ethics, politics, and religion, especially knowledge of what the gods want and how to maintain their favor. Xenophon's Socrates has a similar set of interests, and Xenophon takes pains to defend him

---

2   *Clouds* 142–147, 558–697. Plato, too, observes that there are those who love to learn about certain things (like sights and sounds) who are not possessed of true wisdom or knowledge of the Good (*Republic* 475d).
3   At most they are interested in the political advancement of their pupils (cf. 431–432, 876).
4   At the outset of the *Memorabilia* Xenophon defends Socrates against these charges (1.1.11–16).
5   Cf. Isocrates' speech *Against the Sophists*.

against the criticisms of sophistry.[6] The only appearance of a sophist in the *Cyropaedia* is in the form of Tigranes' tutor (3.1.14). He, however, comes across as interested only in politics and ethics, so much so that he has often been equated with the historic Socrates for the apparent serenity with which he faces death. It is because of the sophist's training that Tigranes is able to convince Cyrus not to execute the Armenian king. And when the sophist himself is being executed by the Armenian king, he serenely counsels Tigranes not to be angry with his father because he had not acted out of malice but out of ignorance (3.1.38).[7]

Learning as a Means to an End

It is not enough for a statesman to *study* subjects relating to leadership. The leader must also be willing to *apply* this knowledge to acts of governance; that is to say, the knowledge of leadership must be a means to an end. Plato intends for the Philosopher King to receive an education that includes both practical knowledge, for example, of warfare, and that is conducive to understanding the Forms of things. The study of mathematics serves both ends (*Republic* 525b). Additionally, the Philosopher King is naturally interested in justice and other virtues because they are a means to understanding the nature of the Good. Yet, as Socrates readily admits, such an interest would not make the Philosopher King want to carry out the daily routines of political life. Even the courageous ruler who is deeply curious about the nature of the *polis* may not want to return to "Plato's cave," as it were, and submit to the labor of command. Only by compulsion or out of gratitude will the Philosopher King actually engage in leading (519c–521a). The true lover of wisdom would not be willing to become sullied by the practice of mundane politics, as he is not a lover of ruling nor a lover of honor. Such a leader would disdain the effort either of fending off those devoted to falsehood (sophists) or of persuading followers with noble lies.

Again, because Cyrus takes pleasure in winning honor and helping others, he is keen to apply his knowledge of leadership to these ends without any societal pressure. And, for another reason we will see below (p. 104), Cyrus does not face the obstacles to governance that the Philosopher King would.

---

[6] That Xenophon could hold a negative view of sophists is clear from his remarks at *On Hunting* 13.8. In the *Cyropaedia*, Araspas blames Eros, the "unjust sophist," for causing him to fall in love with Pantheia, presumably because Eros had given him the tools to rationalize the apparent limitations of his self-control (6.1.41).

[7] There is a textual ambiguity here: it is not clear whether the sophist is assuring Tigranes (1) that his father bears Tigranes no ill will (*kakonoia*) or (2) that his father does not possess ill-will at all because he is acting out of ignorance in believing that the sophist poses a threat to the father. In either case, his "Socratean" serenity is apparent.

Teaching over Manipulation

Cyrus is also not guilty of what many sophists of the late fifth- and early fourth-century were accused of, namely, using their esoteric learning to manipulate their fellow citizens and subvert conventional morality. This problem appears in the *Clouds* when Strepsiades sends his more educable son, Pheidippides, to the Thinkery, where they teach pupils to win arguments by speaking justly and unjustly (98–99). There, Pheidippides learns how to make the good argument sound bad and the bad argument good (112–118). With the confidence that he can behave as he wishes, he denies the existence and authority of Zeus, beats his father, and then sets out to beat his mother (1321–1442).

In the *Cyropaedia*, after Cyrus overtakes the Armenians and puts their king on trial, he then assumes the role of both the prosecutor and judge. Tigranes, educated by a sophist, plays the role of the defendant. Instead of being manipulated, Cyrus, who is trained in matters of justice, listens to Tigranes' points and asks questions along the way. In the end, he does not execute the king but forges a lasting alliance with the Armenians.

Behind the cooperative side of Cyrus' love of learning there seems to be the assumption that a leader cannot manipulate his followers for very long. Manipulation may be a short-term fix to a problem that the group will eventually comprehend.[8] Otherwise, the ruler's trickery will be exposed and he will lose face. As the young Cyrus acknowledges, it is important for a leader to have a reputation for seeming wiser than his followers (1.6.22). When he wonders about the quickest way to win this reputation, Cambyses insists that there is no shorter path to seeming wise than actually being wise. He explains that even if Cyrus should procure fancy clothes and a retinue of people to praise him, he would quickly be exposed as an imposter.

We should pause here and note that Xenophon seems naïve in advancing this view. At the very least, he has idealized the society in which Cyrus operates. Cyrus' Persian peers share his training in matters of justice and thus should be able to detect a specious argument and hold a manipulative leader in check. Are all communities so effective at ferreting out an imposter? Xenophon's Socrates seems to think so: he gives Critobulus the same advice that Cambyses gives Cyrus, that the quickest path to seeming good at something is to be good at it and that it is hard to pretend a reputation for being, say, parsimonious or cautious (*Memorabilia* 2.6.39).

---

[8] Breebaart 1983:120–121 argues that Cyrus' manipulation of his followers in creating a palace for himself in Babylon arises from a monarchical necessity—not from Cyrus' own tyrannical impulse.

Loving Learning without Softness

On the physical and psychological level, a love of learning can seem indicative of cowardice and softness. In the Funeral Oration, Pericles defends the citizens of Athens against this charge when he declares that they love beauty with a purpose and "love wisdom without softness" (cf. Φιλοκαλοῦμέν τε γὰρ μετ' εὐτελείας καὶ φιλοσοφοῦμεν ἄνευ μαλακίας, Thucydides *Histories* 2.40.1). In the *Clouds* young men who spend time studying with sophists are characterized as pale, with sunken shoulders (1015–1019). Socrates' fellow-scholar, Chaerophon, is regularly portrayed as pasty-faced.[9] The Clouds themselves, the play's supreme divinities, even proscribe that pupils refrain from "senseless" gymnastic exercises (417). When Strepsiades burns down the Thinkery at the end of the play, Socrates and his pupils are seen pitifully crying for help (1493–1516).

As we have already seen (p. 32), Xenophon addresses the temptations to luxury and softness from Cyrus' early youth. Cyrus is offered sumptuous meats at his grandfather's Medan table, but passes them up, having been trained in self-mastery (*enkrateia*) in the Persian *agôgê*. The young Cyrus also shows a "killer instinct" both in the hunt and on the battlefield. His curiosity does not lead him down a path of cowardice or physical weakness. Even during symposia and dinner parties, which are the best occasions to indulge in food and pleasure (and to entertain philosophical questions of no practical significance), Cyrus makes sure that his comrades engage in discussion that is both whimsical and serious but always edifying (cf. καὶ γελοῖα καὶ σπουδαῖα, 2.3.1.1). Xenophon says that Cyrus always makes sure that the topics are delightful and conducive to something good (2.2.1.2).

Enriching the Monarchy with Democratic Learning

One point that Plato makes explicitly and implicitly in his writing on leadership is that it requires knowledge and superior intelligence that are not possessed by many members of the community. In the *Statesman*, the Young Socrates and the Eleatic Stranger acknowledge this rarity:

> Stranger: Do you think that any considerable number of men in a particular city will be capable of acquiring the art of Statesmanship?
>
> Young Socrates: That is quite out of the question.

---

[9] *Clouds* 103. Henderson 1988 on this scene notes that Chaerophon was nicknamed "The Bat" for his slender body and pale complexion.

Stranger: In a city with a population of a thousand, could a hundred, say, acquire it satisfactorily—or could fifty, perhaps?

Young Socrates: Statesmanship would be the easiest of the arts if so many could acquire it. We know quite well that there would never be fifty first-class draughts players among a thousand inhabitants—that is, not if they were judged by proper inter-Hellenic standards. How much less can you expect to find fifty kings! For according to our former argument it is only the man possessed of the art of kingship who must be called a king, though he is just as much a king when he is not in power as when he is.

Stranger: You have very rightly recalled that point. I think it follows that if the art of government is to be found in this world at all in its pure form, it will be found in possession of one or two, or at most, of a select few.

Statesman 292e–293a, translation Skemp

It is clear from the surrounding discussion that this "art" of statesmanship consists of a kind of knowledge, like that of a physician or a weaver, of coalescing various members of the state into harmony and friendship (*Statesman* 258b, 311c). Such a statesman, the Stranger explains, can even transcend the law, so long as he acts for the good of the city:

The constitution par excellence, the only constitution worthy of the name, must be the one in which the rulers are not men making a show of political cleverness but men really possessed of scientific understanding of the art of government. Then we must not take into consideration on any sound principle of judgment whether their rule be by laws or without them over willing or unwilling subjects or whether they themselves be rich or poor men.

Statesman 293c, translation Skemp

In the *Republic,* Socrates lays out a plan for the education of the Philosopher King that consists of years of higher-level mathematics, dialectical training, and practical politics, at the end of which is a communing with the Good itself when the Philosopher King is fifty years old (540a). Such a leader will understand the world in a way that no one else, or perhaps only a few other citizens will, necessarily putting himself (or herself) at a distance from the followers.[10]

---

[10] In the *Protagoras,* Plato has Protagoras make the opposite argument that political questions may be decided democratically because all human beings have been invested with a sense of shame

This distancing can have two negative effects. From the ruler's perspective, the followers may seem unworthy to give counsel or instruction. Thus a leader might do as Plato does and strictly divide the community into those whose opinions matter (namely, the rulers) and those whose opinion does not (the guardians and drones). Moreover, the ruler of the ideal state might have to tell noble lies to the guardians and other members of the community.[11]

Or, the leader might behave as the inquisitive Oedipus in Sophocles, who refuses to believe the seer Tiresias when he tells him that Creon is not a threat to him. Oedipus believes that Tiresias is worthless as an advisor because he had been unable to solve the riddle of the Sphinx, whereas Oedipus succeeded by his own native wisdom (*gnomê*).[12] A less rivalrous version of this antithetical relationship exists between the Cyprian king Evagoras and his followers. Isocrates says that in his wisdom Evagoras "had no need of counselors (*sumbouloi*), but nevertheless took counsel with his friends" (*Evagoras* 44).

All of these assumptions about the leader's knowledge and understanding lie at the heart of the justification for monarchical and aristocratic forms of government. Thucydides seems to think it was a positive condition for his city-state that Athens was in name a democracy but in fact ruled by its brilliant first citizen, Pericles (*Histories* 2.65.9). In the famous constitutional debate in Herodotus, seven Persians who have just revolted to reclaim the Persian throne from the Medan imposter discuss the relative merits of democracy, oligarchy, and monarchy. One speaker, Megabyzus, argues against democracy:

> Whatever a tyrant does, he does *knowingly*, but the masses do not know one thing. For how can they know, they who have never been taught nor observed a noble thing for themselves, but rush headlong into their affairs without sense like a river in winter?
>
> Herodotus *Histories* 3.81

From the perspective of the followers, the leader's detachment can look like haughtiness or arrogance, prompting one of the most damning charges in modern politics, elitism. Pericles may have kept company with several sophists and intellectuals of the day (e.g. Damon, Zeno, Protagoras, Aristagoras) and seldom associated with the masses, which gave him a great disdain and contempt for others.[13] Socrates in the *Clouds* is portrayed as literally "up in the

---

(*aidôs*) and right (*dikê*) by Zeus (322c–323c).

[11] Cf. Reeve 1988:183.

[12] *Oedipus the King* 390–403. Oedipus' privileged understanding of the gods is emphasized by the Chorus Leader (*Oedipus the King* 31–57).

[13] Cf. πολλὴν ὑπεροψίαν … καὶ περιφρόνησιν τῶν ἄλλων, *Life of Pericles* 5.3. Stadter 1991a challenges the assumption that Pericles was more affiliated with sophistic teachers than other

air," brought on to the stage by the *deus ex machina*, a device typically used for introducing gods. He first addresses Strepsiades in the condescending manner of a thinker who holds the traditional views of the average Athenian in great contempt.[14]

It would be inaccurate to call Xenophon's Cyrus "democratic" without careful qualification, but he seems more democratic than the leaders in the previous examples vis-à-vis the leader's love of learning.[15] Cyrus is a leader of extraordinary talent, but Xenophon explains that it is "with knowledge" that one comes to secure the willing obedience of one's followers (cf. ἐπισταμένως, 1.1.3.8). As we noted in our discussion of Cyrus' *philomatheia*, this knowledge seemed to be tied more to attentiveness than any special brilliance or esoteric learning (Chapter Two, pp. 51–57). Cyrus does learn the art of divination from his father, but there is no indication that it takes any special skill to do so. As a consequence of this "democratic" view of knowledge, Cyrus regularly asks for and receives intelligence reports from others. He also discusses matters of policy with them and learns from them, as when he listens to the arguments of Tigranes on the benefits of sparing the Armenian king or trusts the Persian commoner Pheraulas to orchestrate a parade of nobles. This is a second advantage to Cyrus' style of leadership over the Philosopher King (the first is his eagerness to lead, p. 99): because Cyrus can learn important information from others (i.e. because Xenophon holds a "democratic" view of knowledge), his leadership is not as lonely or isolated as the Philosopher King's.

Conclusion

Cyrus' *philomatheia* is generally not a problem for him in the ways that it was for other learned leaders of Xenophon's time, whether real or hypothetical. The love of learning for Cyrus is focused on politics and ethics; it is practical, sincere, physically healthy, and fairly democratic. To say that Xenophon portrays Cyrus as "democratic" in his approach to learning is not to say that he completely solves all the problems of the leader's thirst for knowledge in relation to the followers, however. The question of leadership style boils down to the following question: is the knowledge of leadership more like the understanding of multi-variable calculus (as in Plato's ideal city-state) or the skill of planting a healthy crop of grain (as in Xenophon's *Oeconomicus*)? In other words, is the leader's

---

leaders in his day. He proposes the alternative that Pericles gained a reputation for being something of a "Philosopher King" in the wake of Plato's work.

[14] *Clouds* 219ff. In Plato's *Apology*, Socrates regrets that Aristophanes' portrayal gave him such a bad reputation (19b–d).

[15] For further aspects of Cyrus as *dêmotikos*, see p. 35n39.

knowledge *academic* or *agrarian*? If the leader and the follower cannot agree on what knowledge of leading looks like, then it would seem that the ruler is perhaps forced to trade in trust (i.e. his reputation, honor, sincerity) or manipulative story-telling.

6

Three Problems with
Wanting To Be Honored

THE LOVE OF BEING HONORED is the leadership trait in the ancient Greek world that most resembles high-voltage electricity. As we have seen (pp. 76–77), it is a primary source of Cyrus' energy and enthusiasm for leadership, but it may also interfere with the wellbeing of the followers. There is no shortage of examples of the tragic consequences of loving to be honored, and it is the quality that receives the most explicit criticism from Xenophon and other authors, especially from Plato, who has a lengthy critique of the trait in the *Republic*. However much a leader who loves to be honored may sound like a good idea, troubling questions abound: what honors should a leader pursue (all of them?), who should serve as the standard of what is honorable (anyone?), how many risks should be taken to win honor and what kinds (all of them?), by what means should the leader pursue them (by any means necessary?)?

Risking It All—*Carefully*

The leader who is a lover of honor regularly faces a seemingly impossible dilemma. As we have seen in the case of Cyrus' superlative traits (1.2.1), *philotîmia* entails "risking it all," including personal expense, physical health, and mortal safety. It can also entail sacrifices of leisure time and romance. In battle, leaders are often expected to be "first," to put themselves on the frontlines of danger in order to fill their men with confidence and inspiration. At the same time the leader is supposed to care about and plan for the long-term wellbeing of the followers, to be a *philanthrôpos*. In short, the ruler must take greater risks than everyone but do so in such a calculated way as to live long enough to continue to lead. Exactly how to do this is a matter of great import. In a letter to Philip II of Macedon, Isocrates warns the king not to risk himself in the frontlines of battle since his own safety is more important: he must be first in affairs of state more than in the battle charge. In his admonition Isocrates contrasts the prudence of the Persian king Xerxes, who retreated after losing to the Greeks, with the recklessness of Cyrus (not Xenophon's Cyrus), who pursued endless conquest.[1] Isocrates advises Philip to honor a form of courage that does not partake of reckless folly and the "unseasonable love of honor."[2] In the *Memorabilia*, Socrates cautions Glaucon that his love of being honored may ruin him by causing him to think that he can lead the entire city of Athens without ever knowing how to manage a single household (3.6.16).

Anyone familiar with Homer's *Iliad* and *Odyssey* can find instances where a hero places the love of being honored before all else, rushing recklessly into battle or withdrawing out of wounded pride. As the prime example, Achilles withdraws to his tent after Agamemnon deprives him of his war-prize, Briseis, a decision he later regrets because he both fails to help the Achaeans and loses his dearest friend, Patroclus (*Iliad* 18.101–106). Hector, too, in a moment of over-confidence, disregards Polydamas' advice to retreat inside the walls of Troy and prefers the reckless course of dueling with Achilles, a mistake he, too, regrets with shame (*Iliad* 18.285–314, 22.99–110).

Patroclus is an even more interesting case, in that *both* a reckless love of honor and a reckless love for his comrades compel him to storm the walls of Troy against the strict admonition of Achilles (16.89–96), a move that eventually gets him killed. That Patroclus has a concern for his comrades comparable to his desire to win honor is indicated by the prompt medical treatment he gives to the wounded Eurypylus, even though he had been instructed by Achilles only to assess the losses to the Achaean army and return to camp (11.841–848).[3] He later approaches Achilles in Book 16, "weeping like a little girl" for the fallen Achaeans and pleads with Achilles for permission to help them (16.7–19). After he has killed Sarpedon and a number of other Trojans in an intoxicating *aristeia*, he foolishly storms the walls of Troy and is subsequently wounded by Euphorbus, Apollo, and then Hector. Zeus, whose mind is stronger than the resolve of men, robs him of his wits and rouses him to fight (16.684–691).

Perhaps most famously, Odysseus chooses to lead his men into the cave of the godless and unjust Cyclops in hopes that the Cyclops will give him a prize, even though his comrades urge him against it. What's more, upon escaping from the Cyclops' cave, Odysseus proudly taunts Polyphemus (again, against the

---

[1] In Herodotus and Diodorus Siculus Cyrus dies after recklessly attempting to expand his empire.

[2] Cf. φιλοτιμίας ἀκαίρου, *To Philip* 9.1–2. Isocrates makes a similar criticism of the love of honor in the Spartan king Agesilaus (*To Philip* 86–87). Pindar also criticizes "excessive" *philotîmia* as dangerous to the city (Fragment 210). Fourth-century honorific decrees limited the personal benefits of the love of honor by citing the particular beneficiary of the citizen's *philotîmia*, whether it was the city, the tribe, or family (cf. Whitehead 1983:63).

[3] The "leader as healer" is a metaphor used for both Cyrus (*Cyropaedia* 5.4.10) and Alexander (cf. Plutarch *Life of Alexander* 8.1).

protestations of his comrades) and in the process reveals his name, which allows the Cyclops to curse him.[4]

Xenophon would have had many recent and contemporary political figures to draw from for a leader adversely affected by the love of honor or risk-taking. Alcibiades, the fifth-century Athenian statesman and sometime devotee of Socrates, perhaps encapsulates most fully the different problems associated with loving honor.[5] According to Plutarch, when Alcibiades was a boy, he was so focused on winning at knucklebones that he ignored the dangerous approach of a wagon in the street and nearly died (*Life of Alcibiades* 2.3). Most ruinously, Alcibiades convinced the Athenians to make an expedition to Sicily, leading approximately 7,000 of them into slavery (17.1–3). This move was precipitated by the fact that Alcibiades felt that his own reputation was suffering because his rival citizen Nicias had previously negotiated peace with the Spartans.[6]

In his youth, Xenophon's Cyrus shows a reckless pursuit of honor both in the hunt and in his first battle with the Assyrians. When he catches sight of his first animal, he chases it "like someone possessed" and twice almost falls from his horse (1.4.8). Against the Assyrians, he rushes into battle with no consideration for the consequences (cf. ἀπρονοήτως, 1.4.22.8). In what we might call a reckless love of victory (*philonîkia*), he even gloats over the corpses of the men he has killed, to the disappointment of his grandfather (1.4.24). Though he does not later show any other signs of delight in the slaughter, Cyrus does maintain a somewhat reckless impulse to rush into battle: as his comrades prepare to engage the Assyrians, he forgets to march at a walk and takes off on a run, goading the others to join (3.3.62).

In his adulthood, however, Cyrus' love of honor is generally held in check by a habitual caution and attentiveness. Instead of showing his love of victory in battle, he is a lover of victory in the practice of "attentive care" or *therapeia* (8.2.14). Per his father's advice, Cyrus routinely gathers intelligence reports from others and consults the gods before initiating a battle strategy. Nearing the end of his life, he gives thanks to the gods that he always thought "human thoughts" in times of prosperity (8.7.3), a sign that he has learned from the honor-loving folly of his youth.

Though Cyrus does participate in his battles, he is more of a commander than a warrior.[7] He wears glorious armor, but performs no sequence of glorious

---

4 *Odyssey* 9.105–535. On the importance of *philotîmia* in this scene, cf. Friedrich 1991:22.
5 On the sources for Alcibiades' life and their reliability, cf. Rhodes 2011:1–4, 24–25.
6 *Life of Alcibiades* 14.1–9. Cf. Rhodes 2001:39–54, 39–54.
7 By contrast, Isocrates gives Evagoras greater (though still cursory) prominence in the battle when he takes back the throne of Cyprus, perhaps because Isocrates is attempting to mimic poetic conventions of praise (cf. *Evagoras* 30–32).

moments in battle (*aristeia*). The heroic moments of battle are assigned to other characters, notably the husband of Pantheia, Abradatas. His experiences cast Cyrus' love of honor in sharper relief. Like Hector with Andromache in the *Iliad*, Abradatas enjoys a romantic love for his wife.[8] He wins the devotion of Pantheia when Cyrus holds her as a captive (6.1.45) and he proves his devotion when they are reunited. Pantheia fashions armor for him from her own jewelry and sends him into battle against the Assryians with a longing goodbye (6.4.3, 9–11). These gestures, Gera points out, resemble Thetis' gift to Achilles of armor fashioned by Hephaestus and Andromache's parting farewell to Hector in Book VI of the *Iliad*.[9] Though Abradatas has been warned not to hurl himself into the opposing ranks (cf. Achilles to Patroclus, Polydamas to Hector), he rushes recklessly in his chariot into the company of the Egyptians, a position he had won by lot (6.3.36, 7.1.29–32). He sacrifices his life, seemingly out of a desire to win honor, but specifically to repay his debt of gratitude to Cyrus and to impress his wife. After his death his body is mutilated but he is given a monumental funeral with his wife committing suicide over his body (7.3.14–16). His is a reckless but heroic pursuit of honor.[10]

The prince of the Cadusians also pursues the fleeing Assyrians in reckless fashion. He, too, looks for the opportunity to do something remarkable but without first taking counsel with Cyrus or even telling him of the pursuit. His cavalry is subsequently scattered, and he is killed when the Assyrians discover that he has been separated from the army (5.4.16). As usual, Cyrus is gentle and understanding of the prince's recklessness: "what happened was characteristic of humans; for I don't think it strange for those who are human to err."[11] Yet Cyrus also uses the occasion as a "teachable moment," to point out the necessity for thoroughgoing communication among comrades. He insists on a strict network of attentiveness (and self-awareness) not only in the leader but in all the followers as well, to check against the irrational impulses of *philotîmia*.

---

[8]   Delebecque 1978:36, Gera 238–239. On the question of whether the Panthea-Abradatas tale was invented by Xenophon, cf. Perry 1967:169and Gera 1993:245.

[9]   Grea 1993:237.

[10] Cf. Tatum 1989:181–182 and Gera 1993:240–241 on the similarity between Abradatas' tragic and heroic death and that of Xenophon's Cyrus the Younger in the *Anabasis*.

[11] ἀνθρώπινον τὸ γεγενημένον· τὸ γὰρ ἁμαρτάνειν ἀνθρώπους ὄντας οὐδὲν οἴομαι θαυμαστόν, 5.4.17. Cyrus' "human" understanding is a theme in the *Cyropaedia*. Cf. his injunction to Tigranes to forgive his father for killing the sophist on the grounds that his mistake was "human" (ἀνθρώπινά μοι δοκεῖς ἁμαρτεῖν, 3.1.40); and Cyrus' address to Croesus emphasizing that they are both human (ἐπείπερ ἄνθρωποί γέ ἐσμεν ἀμφότεροι, 7.2.5). Cyrus even acknowledges that he is endowed with a lust for wealth, as all humans are (8.2.20).

Pursuing the Right Honors

In Book Five of the *Republic*, Socrates argues that someone who is truly a lover of something loves every aspect of that thing. The most obvious example is that of the lover for his beloved: the lover will consider every feature of the beloved as beautiful, warts and all, despite others who may see imperfection and ugliness (474c). Accordingly, the lover of honor (*philotîmos*) will pursue *any* honor available, high or low. He will settle for being a captain if he cannot be a general. If he cannot be honored by the great and important, he will settle for the small and insignificant.[12] Later, Socrates describes the hierarchy and degeneration of governments, proceeding from aristocracy to timocracy to oligarchy to democracy and then to tyranny. He explains that a timocracy is largely ruled by those whose spirited part of the soul dominates. The spirited part receives guidance from both the rational and the appetitive parts, but over which the rational part does not retain sole dominion. Accordingly, the spirited part of the soul prefers military affairs to dialectic, philosophy, music, and poetry because the love of honor and the love of victory (*philonîkia*) are more important (547–548c; cf. 581a). In a description reminiscent of Xenophon's Cyrus and his interest in the speeches of the sophistically-trained Tigranes, Socrates says that the lover of honor in such a government will love to listen to speeches and argument. Such a leader will base his claim to rule on his physical training, love of hunting, and exploits in war (548e–549a). This person is not bad by nature but highly susceptible to the influence of bad men (550b).

Plato very likely had Alcibiades in mind when he described the *philotîmos* in this way. In a desperate pursuit of *any* honor, Alcibiades boxes the ears of an upstanding citizen for no other reason than that he is goaded to do so by his friends (Plutarch *Life of Alcibiades* 8.1). Plutarch calls him a man of strong passions, but foremost were the "love of contests" and the "love of being first" (cf. τὸ φιλόνεικον, τὸ φιλόπρωτον, 2.1). Plutarch's portrayal of Alcibiades is overall sympathetic, however, because he believes that Alcibiades' beauty, in particular, caused him to be surrounded by flatterers who led him astray and deprived him of the ability to know himself.[13] He was like Plato's indiscriminate

---

[12] *Republic* 475b. Plato knows of exceptions to this rule, such as a person who might crave honor and yet be able to distinguish between good and bad dispensers of honor. He has Agathon in the *Symposium* explain that a speaker is more intimidated at the sight of a few sensible speakers than in the company of many fools (194b). Agathon, who has just won first prize for a tragedy from the Athenians, implies that he would take more pleasure in impressing the wise than the masses.

[13] Xenophon paints a similar, though less sympathetic, picture of Alcibiades (*Memorabilia* 1.2.23).

philotîmos who did not care who did the honoring. It was only in the company of Socrates that Alcibiades was able to moderate his love of honor.[14]

Xenophon describes a similar relationship between the philosopher and politician. As part of his defense of Socrates, he says that Alcibiades and Critias (both pupils of Socrates) surpassed "all Athenians in their love of being honored," which was the ultimate cause of their downfall (cf. φιλοτιμοτάτω πάντων Ἀθηναίων, *Memorabilia* 1.2.12–16). Only in Socrates' company did they show self-restraint (1.2.18), but Xenophon believes that they had the ulterior motive of learning the art of disputation so that they could get the best of their political rivals. They thus abandoned Socrates when they achieved this preeminence.

We may pause here and point out a contradiction to something I said earlier about the fundamentality of the love of being honored to self-restraint and attentiveness. In Chapter Three, I argued that Xenophon seems to think that a leader who loves honor would also be willing to pay attention and check his emotions and physical needs (p. 63). Clearly, Alcibiades loves being honored, but shows little self-restraint except in the company of Socrates. It would seem then that the love of being honored is conducive to self-restraint *only* when the community recognizes this trait as worthy of honor.[15] By contrast, a lover of honor might pursue a lavish lifestyle if those in his company encouraged it.[16]

The fundamentality of the love of honor is even more nuanced than this. While Xenophon says that Cyrus' love of being honored causes him to take risks and toil (1.2.1), such a course of action itself also seems contingent upon a community that values these qualities. When Cyrus proposes that the Persians divide their spoils according to merit, he challenges them to question whether "the man who is willing to undergo the most toil and the most danger is going to meet also with the greatest honor, or do we think that it makes no difference that a man is a coward? For all will meet with equal honors" (2.3.4).

Clearly, *philotîmia* in a leader is not enough to produce virtuous behavior. Successful *philotîmia* requires *both* a community that bestows the right honors *and* (somewhat paradoxically) a leader with enough intelligence (or *philomatheia*) to recognize such a community as well as enough of a concern for the community (*philanthrôpia*) to pursue honors that are beneficial to it. When we say that *philotîmia* is fundamental to Xenophon's Theory of Leadership, we should really

---

[14] *Life of Alcibiades* 4.1–4, 6.1–4. See Whitehead 1983:57–58 on the problems of *philotîmia* in fifth-century Athenian society, particularly as illustrated in Thucydides' analysis of the Peloponnesian War.

[15] We recall that Ischomachus teaches *epimeleia* to the overseers of his estate by rewarding them for it (*Oeconomicus* 12.16).

[16] On the historicity of Alcibiades' reputation as a lavish and promiscuous, see Littman 1970.

say that it is a necessary but *insufficient* part of the foundation, just as sodium is part of the foundation of salt, but by itself does not make food taste better.

Xenophon treats the challenges posed by a flattering community in the example of Croesus, who shows vulnerability akin to Alcibiades'. Croesus allows those around him to convince him that he will become the most renowned general by attacking Cyrus (*Cyropaedia* 7.2.23). He, too, fails to know himself. Cyrus by contrast is very careful in determining which honors to pursue and accept. Ironically, he often wins greater honor by denying initial honors. For example, he does not accept the privilege of making the first spear-cast when he hunts with his Medan age-mates, but wins the admiration of his grandfather (1.4.14). When he departs Media, his kinsmen try to return the presents he had given them, but he declines (1.4.26). When the Armenian king tries to give him more wealth than he had requested, he also refuses. At the height of his power, Gobryas offers Cyrus his kingdom, but Cyrus, refusing this honor, too, finds a way to honor himself even more:

> In turning over to me your fortified walls, manifold wealth, your forces, and your precious daughter, you have made it possible for me to show to all humanity that I am unwilling to be impious or unjust for the sake of gain nor would I willingly violate an agreement.
>
> *Cyropaedia* 5.2.10

In effect, Cyrus construes the act of receiving material honors (e.g. prizes, wealth, property) as a love of gain. By refusing them, he is able to achieve an even higher (mental) honor in the form of the esteem and gratitude of his followers. This principle is also captured well by the Sacian soldier who wins at the horserace in Babylon but will not take a kingdom for his horse; rather he would like the opportunity to "invest in the gratitude (*charis*) of a good man" (8.3.26).

In presenting Cyrus as keeping his own standards of what is honorable, Xenophon draws a strong contrast with the portrayal of Cyrus in Ctesias. Whereas his Cyrus craves approval but also must "approve of the approvers," in Ctesias, Cyrus's ambitions to revolt from Media are continually stoked by his ruthless advisor Oebaras. Challenging Cyrus' self-image, Oebaras says, "there is not a man alive these days who is spirited and noble-minded enough to resolve to overthrow these Medes, who think themselves worthy to rule their betters" and then more forcefully, "perhaps there is someone—only he suffers from a good deal of base cowardice and for this reason does nothing, although he could" (F8d*15). At this point, Ctesias' Cyrus begins plotting his rebellion and relying on Oebaras as a close confidant. Xenophon's Cyrus, however, relies on his own judgment and his knowledge of himself. He is the longed-for marriage between wisdom and power, or between the ambition of an Alcibiades and the sobriety of a Socrates.

Competing Constructively

Perhaps no aspect of *philotîmia* is more problematic than the fact that it can cause leaders to cheat or kill their rivals. Tyrants seldom find ways to stay in power without committing manifold acts of hubris. For example, Periander, the tyrant of Corinth, once received cryptic instruction from the Lesbian tyrant, Thrasybulus. When Periander asked how to deal with unrest in his city, Thrasybulus wandered through the fields of grain, cutting down the tallest stalks, a message to Periander to eliminate his most prominent citizens (Herodotus *Histories* 5.92.ζ). In the famous Constitutional Debate among the Persian conspirators, Otanes disqualifies monarchy from consideration on the grounds that the monarch will always commit acts of outrage out of envy for his peers (Herodotus *Histories* 3.80). As well, Agamemnon's taking of Briseis from Achilles is as much about having a prize as it is about putting Achilles in his place. The leader of the Achaeans says of his challenger, "he wants to be over all of us, to rule all, to lord over all, to give orders to all, but someone I suspect will not obey him" (*Iliad* 1.287-289). We have already noted how Cyaxares is routinely upstaged by Cyrus to his great envy (Chapter Three, pp. 68–69).

Proatês is Cyrus' antidote to envy (see p. 67). He competes with others freely either because he will win or because he knows that he will improve. As a boy, he entertains the possibility of only seeming to be someone impressive rather than actually being it, but his father explains to him that the best way to seem is to be.[17]

Xenophon does not challenge his portrait of Cyrus in every way he might have, though. While it is fair to say that Cyrus is able to compete fairly because of his gentleness and prudence, it is also true that he happens to be the best at everything he attempts. He rides a horse better than all the Medes; he wins a horserace against fellow Persians. He hunts better than everyone both inside his grandfather's wildlife preserve and in the wild. And he fights better in war. He even invites competition among his closest followers in the practice of *therapeia*—and he wins at that, too. Yet Xenophon does not explain how a leader

---

[17] *Cyropaedia* 1.6.22. One place where we might doubt Cyrus' ability to excel others *by being who he truly is* is in his decision to adopt the Medan style of clothing in Babylon, so that it will "charm" his followers (8.1.40–41). Breebaart 1983 argues that the adoption of the Medan style "has nothing to do with the overweening pride of the oriental monarch, it is only the last link in a chain of measures to heighten the status of the aristocracy." For further treatment of Cyrus' adoption of the Medan style, consistent with Breebaart, cf. Azoulay 2004a.

should behave when it becomes apparent that one of the *followers* happens to excel at something. What if a Mede were a better horseman, or a Sacian a better strategist, but did not happen to surpass Cyrus in all categories? It is not clear that Cyrus would or should relinquish power. The closest example of a less competent ruler "stepping aside" is that of Cyaxares, but we have seen the convenience with which Xenophon treats the situation by having Cyaxares show favor to Cyrus since he has no male heirs (8.5.19). Perhaps Xenophon is suggesting that leadership like Cyrus' is so rare in part because it requires a leader to excel in so many different areas. Otherwise, a competitive temperament may ruin the leader and the community of followers. We might even wonder whether Cyrus' successes are possible *only* when the leader excels at all things.[18]

Aside from treating only the case of the thoroughly exceptional leader (Cyrus), Xenophon also does not treat what turns out to be the epistemological problem of determining who is more deserving of a particular honor. The Persian educational system is a meritocracy but one that does not struggle with questions of who is entitled to what honor. Persians employ the best and most senior members of the community who are so versed in justice that they do not seem to question each other's decisions. As Gera notes, Xenophon portrays Cyrus as knowing what he wants and hearing his views echoed back to him from others.[19] Though he does change his mind at times, Cyrus is not required to "love learning" from those who hold opinions that regularly threaten to embarrass him.

Xenophon does deal with this epistemological problem in the *Anabasis*, however, where it is clear that Darius favors his eldest son Artaxerxes II as king, but his queen Parysatis favors Cyrus the Younger (1.1–4). Xenophon himself favors the character of the latter, but in Plutarch it is Artaxerxes II who is seen as the gentle and magnanimous leader struggling to resist his incompetent and treacherous younger brother.

But superlative *philotîmia*, as Xenophon presents it in the *Cyropaedia*, cannot easily be ascribed to a leader who might not happen to be best at everything or who at least might not happen to be *obviously* best. A few observations about the differences between the competitive situations in *Iliad* 1 and 23 will make these limits even clearer. When Agamemnon and Achilles quarrel over Briseis, there are not enough honor-prizes for Agamemnon to be compensated for the loss of Chryseis because, as Achilles points out, they have already been distributed

---

[18] We should also leave open the possibility that Xenophon has given his narrative a fairy tale flavor that is meant to delight his audience more than to instruct them on every challenge of leadership.

[19] Gera 1993:283–284.

(1.125–129). Nor is it obvious who deserves the greater honor or who is in fact the "best of the Achaeans": Agamemnon commands more men, but Achilles is the mightier warrior (1.280–281). When the Achaeans compete in the Funeral Games for Patroclus, however, straightforward contests are set up to see who is best, with the gods often taking a hand. When there are disputes, it turns out that either the disputes are more easily resolved, as with Antilochus and Menelaus (23.596–613); or there are so many prizes to go around that it does not matter much. Nestor even receives a prize without having to compete (23.618–623).

Farber's work on the similarities between Cyrus and Hellenistic kings (as portrayed on inscriptions) sheds further light on how Greeks after Xenophon (and maybe because of Xenophon) sought to deal more carefully with the leader's *philotîmia*. He points out that while *philotîmia* is a praiseworthy trait for kings, it is more often featured in descriptions of excellent royal officials. The hope seems to be that the dangers of *philotîmia* are minimized when the king becomes the *source* (rather than the embodiment) of competitive spirit as well as a judge of each competition. Farber notes further that Xenophon shows a keen interest in the leader's ability to *inspire philotîmia* in the followers, especially in the *Cyropaedia*.[20] In theory, all could go well for the community if the ruler is actually a superior and impartial judge of excellence (i.e. *philomathestatos*).[21] An instance of this practice in the *Cyropaedia* occurs with Cyrus' distribution of honorific seats at dinner, ones that change with time according to the merits of each of his guests (8.4.5). That his comrades have trust in Cyrus' ability to apportion honors fairly is indicated by Pheraulas' support for his apportioning the spoils of battle (2.3.12).

Conclusion

In the foregoing survey of fourteen problems surrounding Cyrus' superlative character traits I have attempted to assess the *comprehensiveness* of what we have been calling the fundamental traits of Xenophon's Theory of Leadership (*philanthrôpia, philomatheia, philotîmia*). This is not to say that these traits are all-encompassing. We have seen cases where Xenophon did not apply his theory to every conceivable circumstance. He does not give much guidance, for example, on how an ambitious leader like Cyrus might "philanthropically" supplant a leader who is not wicked *per se* but is yet unwilling to relinquish authority. Nor does he address competitive situations where the aspiring leader is not superior

---

[20] *Cyropaedia* 8.1.35, 39; 3.3.10, 59. Farber 505.
[21] Cf. Breebaart 1983:128.

in all respects, or where his superiority may reasonably be called into question. Nor does he entertain the possibility that a leader might need to be significantly (and permanently) more intelligent or better-informed than his followers. He offers no advice for a leader whose credibility is called into question by a demagogue who professes a more "common sense" solution. This latter issue is obviously addressed with greater care by Plato, whose Socrates advocates the noble lie to combat just this problem.

Xenophon seems to sidestep certain problems by casting Cyrus in a world that is not perfect, but somewhat idealized or romanticized. The members of his Persian community are largely virtuous or at the very least well meaning, as are many of the leaders he encounters on his adventures. They take the same common-sense ("farmer's") approach to knowledge that Cyrus does. His adversaries are either easily overcome and repentant (the Armenian king, Cyaxares, Araspas, Croesus) or irredeemably wicked, like the Assyrian king, and thus deserving of severe punishment. The conflicts that Cyrus faces in the story are consequently of a much more personal sort: will Cyrus exhibit the proper character to overcome each challenge? Xenophon creates a world in which *some* trait seems to be successful in any given situation.

To say that Xenophon's Theory of Leadership, as it is presented through Cyrus, is not all-encompassing is not to fault him as a thinker inferior to Plato. In some ways his Theory of Leadership is superior: his leader actually wants to lead and takes delight in the success of his followers. The tensions that exist between the two thinkers may be timeless and unresolvable; leadership is an art, not a science, after all. Their theories are better thought of as guideposts for thinking about leadership rather than competing approaches to an absolute or universal notion of ideal leadership. If Xenophon's goal was to tell an entertaining story and to empower would-be rulers to think more carefully about their own leadership, he succeeds quite well.

Finally, the foregoing treatment of these fourteen problems is itself not all-encompassing. Some may find that the problems with Cyrus' superlative traits are more nuanced than I have suggested. Some may find that Xenophon does not solve them as thoroughly as I have claimed. Still others may find additional problems with these traits that are worthy of treatment (there is nothing magical about the number fourteen). What I hope to have set up is a framework and a methodology for understanding Xenophon as a leadership theorist, in such a way that both Classicists and others interested in leadership theory can approach an understanding of a leader's core traits, namely by gauging their *fundamentality* and *comprehensiveness*, features that any good theory ought to have.

Conclusion

THE *EDUCATION OF CYRUS* is a simple narrative, but the Theory of Leadership that informs it is complex and often difficult to untangle. In the course this study I have been exploring a number of claims about it. For one, we should not think of the Theory as a recitation of moral and political commonplaces from a traditional or conservative Greek intellectual. The increasing scholarship on Xenophon over the past thirty years, even when it has not been in consensus, agrees that Xenophon was a lively and serious thinker on the subject of leadership within a host of ancient contexts across time and across cultures. This present work has only reaffirmed this claim and would go further: Xenophon should be at the foundation of any approach to the study of leadership today, as much as Plato, Aristotle, or Machiavelli, whom he either engaged with, anticipated, or heavily influenced. Of particular importance for this study has been the character of the Persian king Cyrus in terms of his three superlative traits, *philanthrôpia*, *philomatheia*, and *philotîmia*.

Meaning

When Xenophon says that Cyrus was celebrated and sung by the Persians for excelling in each of these traits (*Cyropaedia* 1.2.1), he may be reflecting actual Persian lore rather than strictly espousing his own notions of excellent leadership. We may imagine Cyrus' *philanthrôpia* manifesting itself to the Persians in his tendency to spare a conquered enemy, to convert rival kings into counselors, or to host generous banquets where the spoils of the empire are shared with the most needy and most worthy. His *philomatheia* may have appeared in the company of his peers in the Persian educational system (*agôgê*) or in the alacrity with which Cyrus the goatherd (as he is described in Ctesias) worked his way from slave to palace gardener to Astyages' prestigious cupbearer. His *philotîmia* was certainly apparent in his liberation of the Persians from the Medan yoke and his establishment of one of the world's great early empires.

As we saw in Chapter One, these traits (if adapted by Xenophon from Persian tradition) become layered by a number of additional contexts including Xenophon's own ideas as well as those of his fourth-century Athenian contemporaries and the historiographers of Cyrus. *Philanthrôpia* comes to be more than just sparing and sharing, but involves taking sympathetic delight in the success of others and commiserating in their misfortune. It has elements of affection, attentive nurturing (playing the physician), and fondness for the company of others. It has notes of divinity: the powerful leader is advised to emulate the gods who help all human beings with civilizing institutions. Perhaps most importantly from a leadership perspective, *philanthrôpia* involves the practice of "pimping," to use Socrates' term, i.e. matching the interests of others, reconciling and uniting them into more beneficial partnerships, whether marriages or treaties. *Philomatheia* comes to mean more than learning roles and excelling in the *agôgê*. It means paying attention (*epimeleia*) in a comprehensive and tireless fashion. It means taking a natural delight in asking questions, hearing speeches, and being curious. It is a fondness for lessons (*mathêmata*), such as whether it is just to let one boy trade coats with another because the result is more "fitting." *Philotîmia* comes to be more than liberating one's people and winning everlasting glory, also known as *megalopsychia*. It is the desire to fit in, to win the approval and gratitude of one's peers, those in authority, and those who are good people, like Cyrus' father, Cambyses.[1]

Having taken these contexts into consideration in the study of Cyrus' *philanthrôpia*, *philomatheia*, and *philotîmia*, some additional conclusions have emerged. These conclusions are couched, and I think should always be couched, in the cautious language of "seeming" and "suggesting" because the *Education of Cyrus* is for the most part a *story*—not a philosophical treatise or even much of a dialogue. Narration allowed Xenophon to *show*, and thus make his readers *feel* and *reflect on*, what the best leadership looked like without always *explaining* it in technical language. Xenophon almost never states what his Theory of Leadership is, though he may have characters explain aspects of it. Thus his Theory must be inferred from what he says in other works, from what characters do and say in the *Cyropaedia*, from the consequences of their actions, from comparisons among characters, and from comparisons to examples from contemporary and prior literature. We have made particular use in this study of Plato's approach to make *philosophia* the foundation of the Philosopher King's justice, self-restraint, and courage. Accordingly, for Cyrus we have asked to what extent *philanthrôpia*, *philomatheia*, and *philotîmia* are "fundamental" in a conceptual sense to his other

---

[1] In pointing out all of these additional layers to Cyrus' superlative traits from Greek contexts, I am of course not ruling out the possibility that there was also some non-extant Persian context for seeing Cyrus in these additional ways.

leadership traits. We have also made use of the extensive ancient literature on problems of leadership, whether in works of fiction, history, or philosophy.

Distinctiveness

With this methodological framework and the necessary caveats in mind, we may assert with some confidence four conclusions. First, Cyrus' three superlative traits are presented and conceived of as *distinct* features of Cyrus' soul: each of his "loves" is pursued for their own sakes, however much they may operate in conjunction with one another. Xenophon presents them as distinct in his summary statement of Cyrus' character (1.2.1) and with other examples throughout the work. *philanthrôpia* is not merely a *practice* that paves the way for Cyrus to win honor, but an attraction that he *feels* for others in and of itself. The strongest proof of this attraction is the fact that Cyrus frequently shows affection, sympathy, and pity for his followers, as well as pleasure in the act of giving. That these emotions are not merely for show is indicated by the fact that on his deathbed Cyrus takes pleasure in recalling the benefits he has brought to his friends throughout his life. He even hopes to be reunited with the earth in death since both of them are *philanthrôpoi*.

Even though Cyrus tends to "love learning" subjects that are conducive to winning honor (e.g. hunting, warfare, and leadership), Xenophon presents him as naturally curious and alert: as a child he asks about the "causes of things." Finally Cyrus' love of being honored manifests itself in the delight he takes in receiving praise and acceptance from others. This desire to win honor seems to be alloyed with an instinctive desire to compete, to hunt, and to make war on the enemy, even on an irrational level. Thus, *philanthrôpia*, *philomatheia*, and *philotîmia* are distinct features of Cyrus' soul.

All three form an interesting complement to the more famous tripartite division of the soul found in Plato's *Republic*: the appetitive, passionate, and rational parts. Unlike Plato's formulation, where the rational part is expected to dominate the appetitive part and bring the passionate part along as an ally, there seems to be no hierarchy to Xenophon's formulation. It would be difficult to say which of Cyrus' superlative traits dominates his soul. They all seem to be distinct and to enjoy a certain ethical equality, at least as far as the ethics of leadership is concerned.

Fundamentality

Secondly, not only are these traits distinct, but in many ways they are fundamental to other leadership qualities, in the sense that they either play a strong causal role in the creation of these characteristics or they form the fertile ground under which these traits come to be. Thus, for example, Cyrus' love of honor causes him to take risks, restrain himself, endure more, and work harder than those around him. His love of learning and his concern for others make him adept at administering justice. All three traits seem to give rise to his gentleness (*praotês*) and understanding (*suggnomê*). I stress, however, that such derivative traits are not necessarily caused by superlative *philanthrôpia*, etc., but may arise from other sources as well.

Comprehensiveness

Third, these traits are also comprehensive in the sense that Cyrus exhibits them in such a way as to avoid several of their inherent problems. Cyrus loves humanity, but he does so without being manipulated emotionally, without compromising his own interests, without losing discipline within his army or enabling luxuriousness, without inadvertently fomenting a destructive rivalry among his peers or superiors, and without caring so much that he becomes overly stressed. Cyrus loves learning without becoming soft or cowardly, without becoming sophistic or condescending, and without losing his interest to lead. He loves being honored, but not to the point of cheating others or marginalizing them from the competition. He takes risks, but calculated ones. And, as much as he likes winning approval from others, he does not allow *their* standards of what is honorable to control his ambitions; he knows how to recognize a good man or a good woman and seeks to win their favor only.

In saying that these qualities are "comprehensive" I do not mean to imply that I think they are "all-encompassing." Like Newton's Three Laws of Motion or Einstein's Theory of Relativity, they become deficient outside certain parameters of experience. We have noted some problems that Xenophon does not address, for whatever reason, and thus should continue to look for other ways to test and qualify his Theory. Xenophon's Cyrus does not love humanity so effectively that he creates a perfectly meritorious and multicultural empire or appoints the most worthy heir as his successor; instead he appoints his eldest son for reasons of tradition. He does not love learning so much that he studies esoteric subjects that may be relevant to leadership but are nevertheless beyond the comprehension of his followers. Nor is he forced to pursue his love of being honored in contexts where he faces sophistic or manipulative rivals (his rivals in the end are not so formidable). All other accounts of Cyrus' life say that he takes the Medan throne by force, but Xenophon conveniently enables him to win it by his virtues and his devotion to his uncle Cyaxares. Thus by calling Xenophon's ideas on Cyrus' character "comprehensive," I mean to suggest a remarkable attempt on his part to address *many* of the problems inherent in what are seen as otherwise important traits of leadership. I do not mean to say that Xenophon had perfectly worked out every problem of leadership; Xenophon's portrait is not ideal.

Complementarity

Fourth, and somewhat surprisingly, Cyrus' three characteristics are complementary, in that each one tends to hold in check the problems of the other two. Indeed, once this complementarity has been noticed, it is difficult to analyze a scene in the *Cyropaedia* without seeing Cyrus' traits working together; one alone is never sufficient. We might say, simply, that he loves being honored in thoughtful and "philanthropic" ways; or that he cares for others in attentive and honorific ways; or that he loves learning in ways that benefit others and win honor. None of these particular values—love of humankind, of learning, and of honor—is dominant in Cyrus, but instead are coalesced into an apparent harmony, at least as much of one as Xenophon could construct given the constraints of history and the limitations of human character. While they are distinct (as we noted above), they succeed only in conjunction. Simply imagining the fate of a leader who possessed only two of these three superlative traits can give us an immediate and intuitive sense of a precipitous disaster.

Xenophon's Challenges for Us

Given these four features of Xenophon's Theory of Leadership, we can conclude this study by advancing it in two new directions. The first is an obvious one. We have seen that Xenophon takes into account many of the problems of leadership that were current in his time, both at the theoretical and historical level; we have seen that in discussions of leadership Xenophon is just as thoughtful and challenging as his main rival and contemporary, Plato. Nevertheless, we may yet wonder how well his Theory could be applied to the problems of leadership in the modern world. As we noted in the Introduction, Xenophon and his Cyrus have long been part of discussions in the field of political science, but the study of leadership goes far beyond governmental systems. As Xenophon himself knew, leadership was something that also applied to managing a household, teaching a student, treating a patient, and piloting a ship. Similarly, we could wonder how fundamental, comprehensive, and complementary Cyrus' love of humanity, etc. would be in a small business owner, a baseball coach, or the President of the United States. Have we omitted a key ingredient from Xenophon's Theory that we would do well to include; or has his Theory become outmoded in some way?

The second new direction for Xenophon's Theory is rather startling. We noted at the outset and have emphasized here in the conclusion that Xenophon's treatment of Cyrus involves superlatives traits of Cyrus' *soul*, a soul that is capable of distinct aptitudes and loves. While modern neuroscience has not yet found the human soul, it has made fascinating advances in the study of the *brain*. What is interesting for our purposes here is that the brain seems to have many of the same features of Cyrus' soul. The work of Marco Iacoboni and others has brought to light the existence of "mirror neurons," which seem to explain the human capacity to empathize with the pleasures and suffering of others, a feature that we noted was fundamental to Cyrus' *philanthrôpia*.[2] Other work on the neurology of social status has revealed regions of the brain (portions of the prefrontal cortex and the amygdala) that show sensitivity to hierarchy, public failure, and various types of reward.[3] Just as Xenophon thought some souls cared more about winning recognition from others, and that recognition could take various forms (e.g. praise, offices, wealth, and wives), perhaps it is the case that some brains are more sensitive to honor than others, too. Finally, while it goes without saying that the brain (like Cyrus' soul) is the place where the love of learning must occur, scientists are making further advances on aspects of the love of learning, such as attentiveness (*epimeleia*), particularly in studies of ADHD. Dopamine transporters have been seen as crucial to brain functions, like the ability to concentrate or to stay focused on long-term goals, two features we noted were central to Cyrus' leadership.[4]

It would be well outside of my expertise to speculate further on the similarities between recent neuroscience and Xenophon's Theory of Leadership as it pertains to Cyrus' soul, but I raise the connection here as a pathway for future collaboration. It may be that the connections run even deeper than this preliminary sketch; Xenophon may have discovered through observation of human behavior (especially the behavior of children) what scientists can now confirm with functional magnetic resonance imaging. Perhaps future generations will pick leaders using such a Theory as Xenophon's, coupled with brain studies of each candidate, to determine whether or not the candidate actually does love humanity, learning, and being honored to a superlative degree.

---

[2] See Iacoboni's *Mirroring People: The New Science of How We Connect with Others* (2008).

[3] See Zink's "Know your place: neural processing of social hierarchy in humans" (http://www.ncbi.nlm.nih.gov/pubmed/18439411).

[4] See the recent work of Volkow et al. in *JAMA* (http://jama.ama-assn.org/content/302/10/1084.short).

Bibliography

Ambler, W., trans. 2001. *The Education of Cyrus*. Ithaca.

Anderson, J. K. 1974. *Xenophon*. London.

Azoulay, V. 2004a. "The Medo-Persian Ceremonial: Xenophon, Cyrus and the King's Body." In Tuplin 2004:147–17.

———. 2004b. *Xénophon et les grâces du pouvoir*. Paris.

———. 2004c. "Xénophon, la *Cyropédie* et les eunuques." *Revue française d'histoire des idées politiques* 11:3–26.

Bartlett, R., ed. 1996. *Xenophon's Shorter Socratic Writings*. Ithaca.

Bizos, M., ed. 2003. 1971–1978. *Xénophon, Cyropédie*. 5 vols. Paris.

Bonnette, A., ed. 1994. *Xenophon's Memorabilia*. Ithaca.

Breebaart, A. 1983. "From Victory to Peace: Some Aspects of Cyrus' State in Xenophon's *Cyrupaedia*." *Mnemosyne* 36:117–134.

Briant, P. 1996. *From Cyrus to Alexander: A History of the Persian Empire*. Translated by P. T. Daniels. Winona Lake.

Bullough, V. L. 2002. "Eunuchs in History and Society." In Tougher 2002:1–17.

Burian, P. 1974. "Suppliant and Savior: Oedipus at Colonus." *Phoenix* 28:408–429.

Carlier, P. 1978. "The Idea of Imperial Monarch in Xenophon's *Cyropaedia*." In Gray 2010:327–366.

Cook, J. M. 1983. The Persian Empire. New York.

Curtis, J. and J. Simpson, eds. 2010. *The World of Achaemenid Persia: History, Art and Society in Iran and the Ancient Near East*. London.

Danzig, G. Forthcoming. "The Best of the Achaemenids: Benevolence, Self-interest and the 'Ironic' Reading of *Cyropaedia*." In Hobden and Tuplin 2012.

———. 2009. "Big Boys and Little Boys: Justice and Law in Xenophon's *Cyropaedia* and *Memorabilia*." In Gish and Ambler 2009:271–295.

———. 2003. "Did Plato Read Xenophon's *Cyropaedia*?" *Plato's Laws: From Theory into Practice* (eds. S. Scolinicov and L. Brisson) 286–297. Sankt Augustin.

Delebecque, É., ed. 1978. *Xénophon, Cyropédie, Livres 6-8*. Paris.

———. 1957. *Essai sur la vie de Xénophon*. Paris.

De Romilly, J. 1958. "*Eunoia* in Isocrates or the Political Importance of Creating Good Will." *Journal of Hellenic Studies* 78:92–101.

De Ruiter, S. 1932. "De vocis quae est philanthropia significatione atque usu." *Mnemosyne* 59:271–306.

Dillery, J. 1995. *Xenophon and the History of His Times.* London.

Dorion, L. 2010. "The Straussian Exegesis of Xenophon: The Paradigmatic Case of *Memorabilia* IV 4." In Gray 2010:283–323.

Dover, K. J. 1974. *Greek Popular Morality in the Time of Plato and Aristotle.* Cambridge.

Drews, R. 1974. "Sargon, Cyrus and Mesopotamian Folk History." *Journal of Near Eastern Studies* 33.4:387–393.

Due, B. 1989. *The Cyropaedia: Xenophon's Aims and Methods.* Aarhus.

Faber, J. 1979. "The *Cyropaedia* and Hellenistic Kingship." *American Journal of Philology* 100:497–514.

Ferdowsi, A. 1997. *Shahnameh: The Persian Book of Kings.* Translated by D. Davis. New York.

Ferguson, J. 1958. *Moral Values in the Ancient World.* London.

Finkleberg, M. 1998. "*Timê* and *Aretê* in Homer." *Classical Quarterly* 48.1:14–28.

Forster, E. S., ed. 1912. *Isocrates' Cyprian Orations.* Oxford.

Friedrich, R. 1991. "The Hybris of Odysseus." *Journal of Hellenic Studies* 111:16–28.

Gardener, J. 1990. *On Leadership.* New York.

Gera, D. L. 1993. *Xenophon's Cyropaedia.* Oxford.

Gish, D. and W. Ambler, eds. 2009. *The Political Thought of Xenophon.* Exeter.

Goethels, G. and G. Sorenson, eds. 2006. *The Quest for a General Theory of Leadership.* Cheltenham.

Goodenough, E. R. 1928. "The Political Philosophy of Hellenistic Kingship." *Yale Classical Studies* 1:55–102.

Gray, V. 1996. "Herodotus and the Images of Tyranny: The Tyrants of Corinth." *American Journal of Philology* 117.3:361–389.

———. 2007. *Xenophon on Government.* Cambridge.

———, ed. 2010. *Xenophon.* Oxford.

———. 2011. *Xenophon's Mirror of Princes: Reading the Reflections.* Oxford.

Hedrick, L., ed. 2006. *Xenophon's Cyrus the Great: The Arts of Leadership and War.* New York.

Henderson, J., trans. 1988. *Aristophanes'* Acharnians, Lysistrata, Clouds. Newburyport.

Hertlein, F. K., ed. 1886. *Xenophons Cyropadie.* Berlin.

Higgins, W. E. 1977. *Xenophon the Athenian.* Albany.

Hirsch, S. W. 1985. *The Friendship of the Barbarians: Xenophon and the Persian Empire.* Hanover.

Hobden, F. and C. J. Tuplin eds. Forthcoming. *Xenophon: Ethical Principles and Historical Enquiry*. Leiden.

Hutchinson, G. 2000. *Xenophon and the Art of Command*. London.

Jackson, D. F., ed. 2010. *Xenophon's* Cyropaedia: *A Late Byzantine Recension with Facing Page English Tranlsation*. Lewiston.

Jaeger, W. 1942. *Paideia: The Ideals of Greek Culture*. 3 vols. New York.

Johnstone, S. 2010. "Virtuous Toil, Vicious Work: Xenophon on Aristocratic Style." In Gray 2010:137–166.

Kent, R. J. 1953. *Old Persian: Grammar, Texts, Lexicon*. New Haven.

Konstan, D. 1997a. *Friendship in the Classical World*. Cambridge.

———. 1997b. "Friendship and Monarchy: Dio of Prusa's Third Oration on Kingship." *Symbolae Osloenses* 72:124–143.

Kouses, J. and B. Posner. 2007. *The Leadership Challenge*. San Francisco.

Kuhrt, A. 1984. "The Achaemenid Concept of Kingship." *Iran* 22:156–160.

———. 2007. *The Persian Empire: A Corpus of Sources from the Achaemenid Period*. London.

Lefèvre, E. 1971. "The Question of ΒΙΟΣ ΕΥΔΑΙΜΩΝ: The Encounter Between Cyrus and Croesus in Xenophon." In Grey 2010:401–417.

Lenfent, D. 2007. "Greek Historians of Persia." In Marincola 2007:200–207.

Littman, R. J. 1970. "The Loves of Alcibiades." *Transactions of the American Philological Association* 101:263–276.

Llewellyn-Jones, L. and J. Robson, eds. 2010. *Ctesias' History of Persia and Tales of the Orient*. New York.

———. 2002. "Eunuchs and the Royal Harem in Achaemenid Persia (559–331 BC)." In Tougher 2002:19–49.

Lorenz, S. 1914. *De progressu notionis φιλανθρωπίας*. Leipzig.

Mallowan, M. 1972. "Cyrus the Great (558–529 B.C.)." *Iran* 10:1–17.

Marchant, E. C., trans. 1925. *Xenophon's Scripta Minora*. Cambridge.

Marincola, J., ed. 2007. *A Companion to Greek and Roman Historiography*. Oxford.

Martin, H. 1961. "The Concept of *Philanthrôpia* in Plutarch's *Lives*." *American Journal of Philology* 82.2:164–175.

Miller, M. C. 1997. *Athens and Persia in the Fifth Century B.C.* Cambridge.

Mueller-Goldingen, C. 1995. *Untersuchengen zu Xenophons Kyrupädie*. Stuttgart.

Nadon, C. 2001. *Xenophon's Prince*. Berkeley.

———. 1996. "From Republic to Empire: Political Revolution and the Common Good in Xenophon's *Education of Cyrus*." *American Political Science Review* 90.2:361–374.

Newell, W. 1983. "Tyranny and the Science of Ruling in Xenophon's *Education of Cyrus*." *Journal of Politics* 45.4:889–906.

Nikolaidis, A. G. 1980. "A Note on the Relationship between *Philanthropia* and *Humanitas*." *Platon* 63–66:350–355.

Pease, S. J. 1934. "Xenophon's *Cyropaedia*, 'The Complete General'." *Classical Journal* 29:436–440.

Perry, B. E. 1967. *The Ancient Romances: A Literary-Historical Account of Their Origins.* Berkeley.

Pomeroy, S., ed. 1994. *Xenophon's Oeconomicus.* Oxford.

Powell, J. F. G., ed. 1988. *Cicero: Cato maior de senectute.* Cambridge.

Poulakos, T. and D. Depew, eds. 2004. *Isocrates and Civic Education.* Austin.

Rasmussen, P. J. 2009. *Excellence Unleashed: Machiavelli's Critique of Xenophon and the Moral Foundation of Politics.* Lanham.

Reeve, C. D. C. 1988. *Philosopher-Kings: The Argument of Plato's* Republic. Princeton.

Reichel, M. 1995. "Xenophon's *Cyropaedia* and the Hellenistic Novel." In Gray 2010:418–438.

Reisert, J. 2009. "Ambition and Corruption in Xenophon's *Education of Cyrus*." In Gish and Ambler 2009:296–315.

Rhodes, P. J. 2011. *Alcibiades: Athenian Playboy, General and Traitor.* South Yorkshire.

Root, M. C. 1979. *The King and Kingship in Achaemenid Art: Essays on the Creation of an Iconography of Empire.* Leiden.

Sage, P. 1994. "Dying in Style: Xenophon's Ideal Leader and the End of the *Cyropaedia*." *Classical Journal* 90:161–174.

Sancisi-Weerdenburg, H., ed. 1987. *Achaemenid History I: Sources, Structures, and Synthesis.* Leiden.

———. 1985. "The Death of Cyrus: Xenophon's *Cyropaedia* as a Source for Iranian History." In Gray 2010:439–456.

Sandridge, N. 2008. "Feeling Vulnerable but Not Too Vulnerable: Pity in Sophocles *Oedipus Coloneus*, *Ajax*, and *Philoctetes*." *Classical Journal* 103:433–448.

Skemp, J., ed. 1952. *Plato's Statesman.* Bristol.

Stadter, P. 1991a. "Pericles Among the Intellectuals." *Illinois Classical Studies* 16:111–124.

———. 1991b. "Fictional Narrative in the *Cyropaedeia*." *American Journal of Philology* 112:461–491.

Tatum, J. 1989. *Xenophon's Imperial Fiction: On The Education of Cyrus.* Princeton.

Tell, H. 2011. *Plato's Counterfeit Sophists.* Hellenic Studies 44. Washington, DC.

Tougher, S., ed. 2002. *Eunuchs in Antiquity and Beyond.* London.

Tuplin, C., ed. 2004. *Xenophon and His World.* Stuttgart.

———, ed. 2007. *Persian Responses: Political and Cultural Interaction with(in) the Achaemenid Empire.* Oxford.

Weathers, W. 1954. "Xenophon's Political Idealism." *Classical Journal* 49:317–330.

Whitehead, D. 1983. "Competitive Outlay and Community Profit: *Philotîmia* in Democratic Athens." *Classica et Mediaevalia* 34:55–74.

Wood, N. 1964. "Xenophon's Theory of Leadership." *Classica et Mediaevalia* 25:33–66.

Wulf, A. 2011. *Founding Gardeners.* New York.

Index Locorum

Aeschines
  Against Ctesiphon, 138.3, 23n2
  On the False Embassy, 15.8–9, 39
Aeschylus
  Seven Against Thebes, 902, 42n65
  Suppliants, 474–89, 86n8
Aesop
  Fabulae, 62, 81
Apollonius
  Argonautica, 1.7, 36n39; 1.657–701,
    47n5; 2.438–442, 35n37; 2.631–
    637, 94; 2.638, 94n23; 3.66–74, 35,
    3.171–175, 47n5
Aristophanes
  Clouds, 98–99, 100; 103, 101n9;
    112–118, 100; 142–147, 98n2;
    219, 104n14; 417, 101; 431–432,
    98n3; 558–697, 98n2; 876, 98n3;
    1015–1019, 101; 1321–1442, 100;
    1493–1516, 101
  Peace, 371–372, 90; 393, 42n62
Aristotle
  Athenian Constitution, 16.2.4, 66n10;
    16.8.3, 66
  Eudemian Ethics, 1232a19–1233a30,
    27n18
  Nichomachean Ethics, 1123b–1125a,
    27n18; 1155a26–28, 66
  On Virtues and Vices, 1251b1–3,
    39n52
Athenagoras, 2.1.6, 17

Aulus Gellius
  Attic Nights, 14.3, 13n29; 14.3.5,
    49n8

Cicero
  Letters to Quintus, 1.1.23, 8n16
Ctesias, F8d*1–7, 50n9; F8d*5–7,
    23n6; F8d*6–7, 22, 26; F8d*14–19,
    24n10; 26, F8d*15, 113; F8d*22,
    30; F8d*30, 26; F8d*37, 26; F9.8,
    41; F14.43, 24n9;

Demosthenes
  On the False Embassy, 99.1, 39; 139.6,
    39; 140.4, 39
Diogenes Laertius, 3.24, 13
Dionysius of Halicarnassus
  Letter to Gnaeus Pompeius, 4.1.7, 8n16

Euripides
  Andromache, 229, 42n65
  Children of Heracles, 236–46, 86n8
  Hippolytus, 667, 79n1; 730–731,
    79n1; 1034–1035, 79n1
  Medea, 689–745, 86n8
  Suppliants, 334–45, 86n8
Heracleides of Cumae, F2, 32n32

Subject Index

Abradatas: resemblance to Hector, 110

Alcibiades: as a flawed lover of honor, 109, 111–112

Alexander: as a conqueror like Cyrus, 7n13; as a lover of humanity, 43; as a lover of humanity and of Athens, 16–17; as a lover of learning, 98; as incurring rivals because of his generosity, 89; as physician, 31n29; as rival to Philotas, 89n12; high ambition of, 27; problem of proportion with *philanthrôpia*, 87; problematic generosity of, 84; rivalry with Philip of, 91

aspazomai, 24

Assyrian king: envy of, 67–68

attentiveness: as a derivative trait, 69–70

Chrysantas: as a substitute for Cyrus, 37; as more honored than Hystaspas, 87; as obedient and thoughtful, 47; as sharing Cyrus' pleasure in horsemanship, 46n1; as sharing in Cyrus' pleasure in helping others, 38n47

coats: story of, 28, 64–65

Cyaxares: as rival to Cyrus, 90; envy of, 68

Cyrus: apparent manipulation of Cyaxares of, 92–93; as a family member, 23; as affectionate, 23, 38; as non-maternal, 34; as not envious, 67; as playing at king, 22, 24, 27, 28, 44, 53, 90; as playing the role of father, 23; as playing the role of the child, 92; as understanding of human folly, 110; chattiness of, 45; gentleness of, 23; high ambition of, 27; morbid curiosity of in Herodotus, 46; philanthropic deathbed speech of, 40; tears of, 30, 35, 91; treatment of the eunuch Gadatas of, 40–41

Cyrus the Younger, 3, 5, 41, 48, 55, 91

dikaiosunê: as a derivative trait, 64–66; limits for Cyrus, 87–88

enkrateia, 32, 63

Lightning Source UK Ltd.
Milton Keynes UK
UKHW02f2324170818
327352UK00006B/615/P